First World War
and Army of Occupation
War Diary
France, Belgium and Germany

35 DIVISION
106 Infantry Brigade
Highland Light Infantry
12th (Service) Battn
1 February 1918 - 29 April 1919

WO95/2490/1

The Naval & Military Press Ltd
www.nmarchive.com
Published in association with The National Archives

Published by

The Naval & Military Press Ltd

Unit 10 Ridgewood Industrial Park,

Uckfield, East Sussex,

TN22 5QE England

Tel: +44 (0) 1825 749494

www.naval-military-press.com

www.nmarchive.com

Contents

Document type	Place/Title	Date From	Date To
Heading	WO95/2490/1		
Heading	35th Division 106th Infy Bde 12th Bn Highland Lt Infy Feb 1918 Apr 1919 From 15 Div 46 Bde		
War Diary	Bernville	01/02/1918	03/02/1918
War Diary	In The Line	04/02/1918	09/02/1918
War Diary	Elverdinghe	10/02/1918	16/02/1918
War Diary	In The Line	16/02/1918	23/02/1918
War Diary	Canal Bank	24/02/1918	24/02/1918
War Diary	Canal Camp	25/02/1918	28/02/1918
Heading	106th Inf. Bde. 35th Div. War Diary 12th Battn. The Highland Light Infantry. March 1918 Attached:- Narrative Of Operations 23rd to 30th March		
War Diary	Canal Bank Near Boesinghe	01/03/1918	01/03/1918
War Diary	Elverdinghe	01/03/1918	07/03/1918
War Diary	Langemarck & Front Line-V 7 B rd	07/03/1918	08/03/1918
War Diary	Front Line in V 7 b & d	09/03/1918	09/03/1918
War Diary	Boesinghe	10/03/1918	10/03/1918
War Diary	International Corner	10/03/1918	10/03/1918
War Diary	J Camp near Peselhoek	10/03/1918	10/03/1918
War Diary	J Camp Peselhoek	14/03/1918	23/03/1918
War Diary	Proven	24/03/1918	24/03/1918
War Diary	Bray	24/03/1918	24/03/1918
War Diary	Bois Adviere near Maricourt	24/03/1918	25/03/1918
War Diary	Maricourt	25/03/1918	26/03/1918
War Diary	Buire	26/03/1918	26/03/1918
War Diary	Lavieville	27/03/1918	27/03/1918
War Diary	Buire	27/03/1918	28/03/1918
War Diary	Lavieville	27/03/1918	27/03/1918
War Diary	Buire	27/03/1918	29/03/1918
War Diary	Near Buire	30/03/1918	30/03/1918
War Diary	La Neuville	30/03/1918	31/03/1918
Miscellaneous	12th Battalion Highland Light Infantry Narrative of Operations 23/3/18	23/03/1918	23/03/1918
Miscellaneous	War Diary		
Miscellaneous	12th Battalion Highland Light Infantry Orders By Major W.H. Anderson 6th March 1918	06/03/1918	06/03/1918
War Diary	Heilly	01/04/1918	05/04/1918
War Diary	In The Line	06/04/1918	11/04/1918
War Diary	Hedauville	12/04/1918	14/04/1918
War Diary	In The Line	15/04/1918	23/04/1918
War Diary	Aveluy Wood	24/04/1918	30/04/1918
Diagram etc	Rough Sketch Map Showing dispositions 12th High L.I. 10.4.18		
Operation(al) Order(s)	106th Brigade Order No. 12		
War Diary	Rubempre	01/05/1918	03/05/1918
War Diary	In The Line	04/05/1918	08/05/1918
War Diary	Robempre	09/05/1918	18/05/1918
War Diary	In The Line	19/05/1918	31/05/1918
War Diary	Forceville	01/06/1918	01/06/1918
War Diary	Aueluy Wood.	02/06/1918	16/06/1918

War Diary	Warloy	17/06/1918	17/06/1918
War Diary	Argueves	18/06/1918	30/06/1918
War Diary	Arqueves	01/07/1918	01/07/1918
War Diary	Zermazeele	02/07/1918	04/07/1918
War Diary	Near Steenvoorde	04/07/1918	08/07/1918
War Diary	In Reserve S/27. Q. 11 Central	09/07/1918	12/07/1918
War Diary	In The Line	12/07/1918	12/08/1918
War Diary	Steenvoorde	13/08/1918	01/09/1918
War Diary	En Route	02/09/1918	02/09/1918
War Diary	Road Camp	03/09/1918	03/09/1918
War Diary	Line	04/09/1918	06/09/1918
War Diary	In The Line	06/09/1918	06/09/1918
War Diary	Poperinghe	07/09/1918	15/09/1918
War Diary	Kruisstraat	16/09/1918	28/09/1918
War Diary	In The Line	28/09/1918	30/09/1918
Operation(al) Order(s)	12th Battalion Highland Light Infantry Operation Order No. 34	03/09/1918	03/09/1918
Operation(al) Order(s)	12th Battalion Highland Light Infantry. Operation Order No. 36	08/09/1918	08/09/1918
Miscellaneous	Operation Orders		
War Diary	In The Line	01/10/1918	03/10/1918
War Diary	Kruisstraat Area	04/10/1918	05/10/1918
War Diary	Kruisstraat	06/10/1918	09/10/1918
War Diary	In The Line	10/10/1918	28/10/1918
War Diary	Courtrai	28/10/1918	29/10/1918
War Diary	In The Line	30/10/1918	31/10/1918
Operation(al) Order(s)	12th Battalion Highland Light Infantry Report On Operations	27/09/1918	27/09/1918
Miscellaneous	12th Battalion Highland Light Infantry Narrative of Operations 14-10-18	14/10/1918	14/10/1918
War Diary	In Reserve Knocke	01/11/1918	01/11/1918
War Diary	Belleghem	02/11/1918	06/11/1918
War Diary	Courtrai	07/11/1918	11/11/1918
War Diary	Leynstraat	11/11/1918	15/11/1918
War Diary	Nukerke	16/11/1918	19/11/1918
War Diary	Harle Beeke	20/11/1918	30/11/1918
Miscellaneous	12th Highland Light Infantry.	29/11/1918	29/11/1918
Miscellaneous	12th Highland Light Infantry.	30/11/1918	30/11/1918
Miscellaneous	Strength Return.	30/11/1918	30/11/1918
Miscellaneous	Column "B"		
War Diary	Wulverdinghe	01/12/1918	01/12/1918
War Diary	Houlle	02/12/1918	06/12/1918
War Diary	Millam	07/12/1918	31/01/1919
War Diary	Millam	01/01/1919	29/01/1919
War Diary	Calais	30/01/1919	31/01/1919
War Diary	Millam	01/02/1919	01/04/1919
War Diary	Tilques	11/04/1919	18/04/1919
War Diary	Dunkirk	19/04/1919	29/04/1919
Miscellaneous	A.A Positions & Mountings		

35TH DIVISION

106TH INFY BDE

12TH BN HIGHLAND LT INFY

FEB 1918-APR 1919

FROM 15 DIV

46 BDE

Instructions regarding War Diaries and Intelligence Summaries are contained in F. S. Regs., Part II. and the Staff Manual respectively. Title pages will be prepared in manuscript.

WAR DIARY
or
~~INTELLIGENCE SUMMARY.~~

(*Erase heading not required.*)

12TH. HIGH. L. I. For February 1918.

106/35 Army Form C. 2118.

Vol 25 196

Place	Date	Hour	Summary of Events and Information	Remarks and references to Appendices
BERNVILLE	1918 FEBY 1		Battalion in Billets. Companies carry out Musketry on Various Ranges.	
	2		ditto Companies at the disposal of Company Commanders. MAJOR J. A. COX assumes the duties of 2nd in command. 2/LIEUT. J. INGLIS joins the Battalion & is posted to "A" Coy. Intimation received that Batt. joins 35th Div.	
	3		Battalion marches to BEAUMETZ STATION & entrains at 12.30 pm. for PESELHOEK. arriving & detraining at 10.30 pm. Battalion is marched to hutted camp by Bands of 17th Royal Scots & 18th H.L.I. Detraining completed & Battalion settled in camp by 2 A.M. Batt. is sent to 106th Brigade	Feb 18 / Apr 19
IN THE LINE	4		Weather clear & dry & milder than in ARRAS sector. The Battalion moves into Divisional Reserve, moving by rail to HILLTOP CAMP, where the men are accomodated in NISSEN HUTS. Only 4 Officers & 40 men per Coy. ARB move with the Battalion, the remainder of the Officers & men remain at Details Camp under command of Capt. Johnstone.	
	5		Battalion in huts as above. Day passes without incident. Artillery engaged on both sides in Counter-Battery Work.	

A5834 Wt. W4973 M687 750,000 8/16 D. D. & L. Ltd. Forms/C.2118/13.

Army Form C. 2118.

Instructions regarding War Diaries and Intelligence Summaries are contained in F. S. Regs., Part II. and the Staff Manual respectively. Title pages will be prepared in manuscript.

WAR DIARY
or
INTELLIGENCE SUMMARY.
(*Erase heading not required.*)

197

Place	Date	Hour	Summary of Events and Information	Remarks and references to Appendices
	1918			
IN THE LINE	FEBY 6		Battn in BRIGADE RESERVE as above and accomodated in HUTS in HILLTOP CAMP.	
	7		do. Working Parties supplied employing about 100 men. Weather wet & disagreeable	
	8		Battn in Huts as above. Companies employed in draining & cleaning up camp.	
	9		Battalion is relieved by 1st Black Watch, & proceed by march Route to Rest Billets at ELVERDINGHE, arriving at 12 noon.	
ELVERDINGHE	10		Battalion in Hutted Camp. Training carried out in neighbourhood of camp.	
	11		Battalion in Hutted Camp SOUTH of ELVERDINGHE. Draft of 75 O.R. & 2 Officers report for duty. Officers are posted to Companies as follows:- 2/LIEUT. C. J. HARRIS to B Company. D. J. REOCH to D Company. Orders are received to move to LARREY CAMP, which move was completed & Battalion established in New Camp by midday.	[illegible]

A7092 Wt W128 9/M1293 750,000. 1/17. D. D & L., Ltd. Forms/C2118/14.

Instructions regarding War Diaries and Intelligence Summaries are contained in F. S. Regs., Part II. and the Staff Manual respectively. Title pages will be prepared in manuscript.

WAR DIARY
or
INTELLIGENCE SUMMARY.
(*Erase heading not required.*)

Army Form C. 2118.

198

Place	Date	Hour	Summary of Events and Information	Remarks and references to Appendices
ELVERDINGHE	1918 FEB 12		Battalion in Hutted Camp at LARREY FARM.	
	13		Battalion parade for inspection by Brigadier General Commanding 106th Infantry Brigade. Weather very wet & unfavourable.	
	14		Battalion in billets as above. Training carried out in vicinity of camp. Weather dry but ground very muddy. 2/LIEUT. C. MILLER proceeds to join M.G.C. & is struck off the strength.	
	15		Battalion in Camp as above. G.O.C. 35th Division inspects two Companies in full Marching Order drawn up on Football Field adjoining LARRY CAMP. G.O.C. gives a short address of welcome & expresses his satisfaction at the appearance of the men.	
	16		Battalion moves into the Line taking over the RIGHT Sub-Sector of the Divisional Front. Companies are conveyed by train from LARREY CAMP to KEMPTON PARK station, & thence the move is by March Route.	[signature]

A7092 Wt. W128 9/M1293 750,000. 1/17. D. D & L., Ltd. Forms/C2118/14.

Army Form C. 2118.

199

Instructions regarding War Diaries and Intelligence Summaries are contained in F. S. Regs., Part II. and the Staff Manual respectively. Title pages will be prepared in manuscript.

WAR DIARY
or
INTELLIGENCE SUMMARY.
(Erase heading not required.)

Place	Date	Hour	Summary of Events and Information	Remarks and references to Appendices
~~to~~ IN THE LINE	1918 FEB. 16		Companies are disposed as follows "B" Coy. RIGHT FRONT, "D" Coy LEFT FRONT, "C" Coy. SUPPORT, "A" Company RESERVE.	
			Owing to lack of accomodation in the Front Line the two Companies holding the LINE are limited in numbers to 80 O.R. each. SUPPORT & RESERVE COYS have additional personnel attached, 40 & 20 respectively accomodated with the RESERVE Company in EAGLE TRENCH. These are used for Working Parties.	
			SUPPORT Company Dispositions are as follows:-	
			COY. H.Qrs. at OLGA HOUSES, one Officer & one platoon & a half in KANGAROO HOUSES for Counter-Attack purposes, & remainder of Company as permanent garrison in EAGLE TRENCH.	
			RESERVE Company in EAGLE TRENCH. Battn H.Qrs. in SOUVENIR HSE.	
			The Line taken over & the relief of the 19th Durham Light Infantry completed by 10 pm.	
	17		Battalion holding the Line as above. Weather dry and cold. Situation quiet	[initials]

A7092. Wt. W128 9/M1293 750,000. 1/17. D. D & L., Ltd. Forms/C2118/14.

Instructions regarding War Diaries and Intelligence Summaries are contained in F. S. Regs., Part II. and the Staff Manual respectively. Title pages will be prepared in manuscript.

WAR DIARY
or
INTELLIGENCE SUMMARY.
(Erase heading not required.)

Army Form C. 2118.

200

Place	Date	Hour	Summary of Events and Information	Remarks and references to Appendices
~~19~~	1918			
IN THE LINE	FEB. 17		Artillery active on both sides. M.G. opposite our front traverse front & Support Lines during night.	
	18		Battn. holding the Line as above. Situation quiet. Considerable activity on the part of enemy Artillery. During the afternoon the area of the RESERVE Coy. near EAGLE TRENCH was subjected to a heavy bombardment by 8" shells, about 150 shells landing in its immediate vicinity. In retaliation for a raid carried out by our troops on the left, the area occupied by the Battn. was subjected to fairly heavy shelling. One enemy aeroplane was observed to crash in neighbourhood of HOUTHULST FOREST, brought down by one of our machines. Inter-Company relief carried out, the new dispositions being as follows:- RIGHT Company "C" Coy. LEFT Company "A" Coy.	[illegible initials]

A7092 Wt. W128 9/M1293 750,000. 1/17. D. D & L., Ltd. Forms/C2118/14.

Army Form C. 2118.

WAR DIARY
or
INTELLIGENCE SUMMARY.
(Erase heading not required.)

Instructions regarding War Diaries and Intelligence Summaries are contained in F. S. Regs., Part II. and the Staff Manual respectively. Title pages will be prepared in manuscript.

201

Place	Date	Hour	Summary of Events and Information	Remarks and references to Appendices
IN THE LINE	1918 FEBY. 19		SUPPORT Coy. "D" Coy. Reserve Company "B" Company. Relief completed by 10 pm.	
	20		Battalion in the Line as above. Weather cold and damp. Situation quiet. Several gas shells fired by hostile artillery landed in neighbourhood of Support Companies H.Qrs.	
	21		Battalion in line as above is relieved by the 18th. H.L.I. moving into Support with H.Qrs at PIG & WHISTLE.	
	22		Battalion in Brigade Support as above. Situation quiet throughout the day except for heavy hostile shelling NORTH of Battn. H.Qrs. Weather damp and cold.	
	23		Battalion in Support is relieved by the 4th North Staffords & on relief proceed by march route two Companies & H.Qrs. to CANALBANK CAMP & two Companies to CAMBRIDGE CAMP. Battalion all settled in respective Camps by 11 pm. ~~Casualties RB~~ ~~during tour 4 O.R. Wounded RB~~	
CANALBANK	24		Battalion in dug-outs. Cleaning & inspections carried out by Companies. Total casualties for the tour 1 Killed & 5 Wounded.	[signature]

A7092 Wt W128 9/M1293 750,000 1/17 D. D & L., Ltd. Forms/C2118/14.

Instructions regarding War Diaries and Intelligence Summaries are contained in F. S. Regs., Part II. and the Staff Manual respectively. Title pages will be prepared in manuscript.

WAR DIARY
or
INTELLIGENCE SUMMARY.
(Erase heading not required.)

Army Form C. 2118.

207

Place	Date	Hour	Summary of Events and Information	Remarks and references to Appendices
CANAL CAMP	1918 FEBY. 25		Battalion in Dug Outs in Canal Bank. Weather dull & unsettled. "C" Company moves from CAMBRIDGE CAMP to CANAL CAMP. 2/LIEUT. T. FORSYTH joins the Battalion for duty & is posted to "A" Coy. 2/LIEUT. J. INGLIS proceeds to join the R.F.C. & is struck off the strength. Battalion has baths & a clean change of underclothing.	
	Feby 26th		Battalion supplies Working Party of 7 officers and 350 O.R. for work on the Army Line. Major W. H. ANDERSON having rejoined from two months leave takes over command of the Battalion.	
	Feb 27th		Battalion again supplies Working Party of 7 officers and 350 O.R. The Remainder carrying on training. More accomodation now being available in the Canal Bank "D" Coy is moved up from CAMBRIDGE Camp and reports move complete by 6 p.m. The whole Battalion is now accomodated in the Canal Bank except the Quartermasters Stores and Transport which remain permanently at ELVERDINGHE. 2/Lt. J. Hope reports for duty & is posted to "C" Coy.	
	Feb 28th		A Working party of 7 officers & 350 O.R. is supplied remainder of the Battalion training. Great air activity in evening owing to clear calm weather.	[illegible]

W H Anderson Major
Comnd. 12. H.L.I.

A7092 Wt. W128 9/M1293 750,000. 1/17. D. D & L., Ltd. Forms/C2118/14.

106th Inf.Bde.
35th Div.

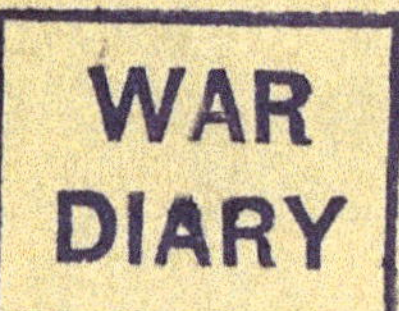

12th BATTN. THE HIGHLAND LIGHT INFANTRY.

M A R C H

1 9 1 8

Attached:-

Narrative of Operations
23rd to 30th March.

Instructions regarding War Diaries and Intelligence Summaries are contained in F. S. Regs., Part II. and the Staff Manual respectively. Title pages will be prepared in manuscript.

WAR DIARY
or
INTELLIGENCE SUMMARY.
(Erase heading not required.)

Army Form C. 2118.

12 H.L.I

MARCH 1918

106/35

Vol 28

Place	Date	Hour	Summary of Events and Information	Remarks and references to Appendices
CANAL BANK NEAR		0.00 a.m. to 2.30 p.m.	Battalion still in Divl Support	
BOESINGHE	1/3/18	–	Battalion moved as part of 106 INF BDE. into (35th) Divl Reserve to LARREY CAMP near ELVERDINGHE	
	– " –	2.30 pm	Starting Point + Rds at B 12.d 3.4. – Route via ~~[illegible]~~ – CHEAPSIDE – DAWSON CORNER – ELVERDINGHE.	
	– " –		Usual march routine was observed – Bn was relieved in Support by 2nd N STAFFORDSHIRE REGT	
ELVERDINGHE	– " –	5.0 pm	Battalion arrived at LARRY CAMP without incident.	
– " –	2/3/18	–	Battalion supplied a working party of 7 Officers 353 O.R. under Lt GILCHRIST ~~for~~ C.R.E. Army Zone on Army Line. Party entrained at ~~[illegible]~~ ELVERDINGHE at 8.15 a.m. and returned to Camp at 6 p.m. –	
			Working Party of 20 O.R. also supplied to 183rd TUNNELLING Coy at HULLS FARM for [illegible]	
			1 N.C.O. & 2 men also supplied to II Corps School for Demonstration Platoon	
			Remainder of battalion occupied in Specialist training.	
– do –	3/3/18	–	Battalion occupied in Church Parades. Lectures & Baths during the day	
– do –	4/3/18	7.25 a.m.	Battalion "stood by" for a CONTACT AEROPLANE Demonstration – Cancelled at 8.a.m. owing to unfavourable weather – Remainder of day spent in Coy training.	

28.M.
18 sheets

2353 Wt. W2544/1454 700,000 5/15 D. D. & L. A.D.S.S./Forms/C. 2118.

Instructions regarding War Diaries and Intelligence Summaries are contained in F. S. Regs., Part II. and the Staff Manual respectively. Title pages will be prepared in manuscript.

WAR DIARY
or
INTELLIGENCE SUMMARY.
(Erase heading not required.)

Army Form C. 2118.

Place	Date	Hour	Summary of Events and Information	Remarks and references to Appendices
ELVERDINGHE	5/3/18	1.30 a.m.	Battalion Stood to at 1.30 a.m. for warning order to man its allotted place in Army Battle Zone in U 28. area (~~Ref~~ Map. BELGIUM 20.S.W. S.E. 1/40000) -	
		3.45 a.m.	Received orders to move off - Battalion formed up on road at CARREY CAMP and moved at 4.0 a.m. via BOESINGHE. ~~[illegible]~~ & "A" TRACK, moving in artillery formation after crossing YPRES CANAL - Dispositions - Bn HQ STRAY Fm. (nr. PILKEM) 'A' Coy left front (U 28 b) 'B' Coy left support (U.28.c) 'C' Coy Right front (U 28. d) 'D' Coy Reserve (in BATTERY COPSE area) - All positions formed & manned by 6.30 a.m.	
		9.0 a.m.	Battn withdrew under orders from Bde. - to CARRY CAMP. via ~~[illegible]~~ IRON CROSS - PILKEM & BOESINGHE in very small parties owing to daylight & visibility	
		10.30 a.m.	Battn arrived back at CARREY CAMP - Remainder of day spent in Lectures &	
- do -	6/3/18	7.30 a.m.	Battalion marched to CANAL BANK for Contact Aeroplane Demonstration - This was cancelled on arrival at BOESINGHE owing to mist. 2nd i/c reconnoitred Right Bn. Sector of Divl. Front.	
		10. a.m.	Battn arrived back in Camp & occupied in Inspections &	

2353 Wt. W2544/1454 700,000 5/15 D. D. & L. A.D.S.S./Forms/C. 2118.

Instructions regarding War Diaries and Intelligence Summaries are contained in F. S. Regs., Part II. and the Staff Manual respectively. Title pages will be prepared in manuscript.

WAR DIARY
or
INTELLIGENCE SUMMARY.
(Erase heading not required.)

Army Form C. 2118.

Place	Date	Hour	Summary of Events and Information	Remarks and references to Appendices
ELVERDINGHE	7/3/18	am	Battalion cleaned up camp & marched to ELVERDINGHE STATION at midday to entrain for KEMPTON PARK.	
LANGEMARCK & FRONT LINE in V.7.b & d.	— " —	pm	Battalion relieved 18th LANCS FUSRS in Right Sub-sector of Centre Divl. front of II Corps. "B" Coy relieving "Z" Coy of 18th L.F., [illegible] as Right Front Coy, "C" Coy relieving "Y" Coy as Left Front Coy, "A" Coy relieving "X" Coy in Support, "D" Coy relieving "W" Coy in Reserve – The night passed with lively enemy shelling of front & support systems – 3 casualties to "C" Coy & one to "B" Coy –	"A"
— do —	8/3/18	—	Enemy attacked Left Divl. front near HOUTHULST FOREST – & shelled our front line posts no progress for enemy. Intermittent artillery & M.G. activity all day. At night our Coys busy on strengthening existing defences & wiring their front. Each Coy sent out fighting patrols but enemy avoided contact. Enemy artillery very active at night ~~[illegible]~~ New medical aid Post formed at IMBROS HOUSE (V.18.d.6.1). Battn. H.Q. at SOUVENIR HOUSE was commenced as a Strong Point to be held by 30 O.R. in addition to being Bn. H.Q.	

Army Form C. 2118.

Instructions regarding War Diaries and Intelligence Summaries are contained in F. S. Regs., Part II. and the Staff Manual respectively. Title pages will be prepared in manuscript.

WAR DIARY
or
~~INTELLIGENCE~~ SUMMARY.
(Erase heading not required.)

Place	Date	Hour	Summary of Events and Information	Remarks and references to Appendices
Front line in V 7 b & d	9/3/18	—	Intense enemy artillery fire on our front areas all day in connection with operations of Left Div at HOUTHOULST FOREST – Support Coy & Bn. HQ were shelled with gas shell – especially in valley of LAUDETBEEK – Very few casualties however – Usual work on Coy areas – New strong point at Bn. H.Q. strongly wired.	
		9.30p	Battalion was relieved by 1st LOYAL NORTH LANCS. REGT & marched back to entrain at BOESINGHE STATION.	
BOESINGHE	10/3/18	0.5 a.m.	Entrained at BOESINGHE STATION for INTERNATIONAL CORNER.	
INTERNATIONAL CORNER		1.30 a.m.	Battn detrained and proceeded to J Camp near PESELHOEK.	
J Camp near PESELHOEK			Battn occupied in cleaning up – overhauling &c.	
— do —	11/3/18		Battn occupied in ~~Coy~~ training under Coy arrangement	
— do —	12/3/18		— Parades as for 11th inst, – Battn played 18th H.L.I. at football —	
— do —	13/3/18		Parades as for 12th inst – Working party under Bde of 1 Offr & 100 OR. supplied for local improvements.	

Instructions regarding War Diaries and Intelligence Summaries are contained in F. S. Regs., Part II. and the Staff Manual respectively. Title pages will be prepared in manuscript.

WAR DIARY
or
INTELLIGENCE SUMMARY.
(Erase heading not required.)

Army Form C. 2118.

Place	Date	Hour	Summary of Events and Information	Remarks and references to Appendices
J. CAMP nr PESELHOEK	14/3/18	–	Battalion occupied in training & baths – all rifles overhauled. C.O. inspected Bn kits	
– do –	15/3/18		~~As for 14th~~ all available officers & O.R. of Battn at work on Army Zone under R.E. from 6.20 a.m. to 5 p.m. (including time moving to & from) Major W.H. Anderson authorised by G.O.C. 35th Div to wear badges of Lieut-Colonel. Major J.A. Cox assumed temporary command of the battalion at 7 p.m.	
– do –	16/3/18		Working parties as for 15/3/18. Divine Service for surplus O.R. Detachment of 1 officer & 20 O.R. attended Army Commander's Inspection as part of 106 INF. BDE. party	
– do –	17/3/18		Working parties as for 15/3/18.	
– do –	18/3/18		Working parties as for 15/3/18.	
– do –	19/3/18		Working parties as for 15/3/18. Battn won Brigade Stretcher Bearers Competition	
– do –	20/3/18		——— do ———	

Army Form C. 2118.

Instructions regarding War Diaries and Intelligence Summaries are contained in F. S. Regs., Part II. and the Staff Manual respectively. Title pages will be prepared in manuscript.

WAR DIARY
or
~~INTELLIGENCE SUMMARY.~~
(Erase heading not required.)

Place	Date	Hour	Summary of Events and Information	Remarks and references to Appendices
"J" CAMP near PESELHOEK	21/3/18	—	Working Parties as for 15/3/18. Lt Col. W.H. Anderson returned & took over command of Bn.	
			Camp was shelled all day & night by enemy 8" long range gun	
— . —	22/3/18		Battalion engaged in cleaning parades – Camp site shelled by enemy H.V. gun.	
— . —	23/3/18	6.0 a.m.	Battn marched to PROVEN for entrainment	
PROVEN	— . —	9.0 a.m.	Battn entrained & proceeded via CALAIS – BOULOGNE – ETAPLES – ABBEVILLE & AMIENS to HEILLY where it detrained and marched to BRAY SUR SOMME	
BRAY –	24/3/18	7.0 a.m.	Battn marched to MARICOURT to wait for battle-action.	
		12.0.	Battn marched to HARDECOURT AU BOIS and with 2 Coys under Major J.A. COX attacked the HARDECOURT RIDGE, which was occupied with little loss.	
			After capture orders were sent by ~~Brigade~~ 9th Div to evacuate the ridge & retire to HARDECOURT – ('A' Coy covered withdrawal –) as no troops could be got to cover our flanks in time.	'B'
			Battn occupied outpost line astride the HARDECOURT – MARICOURT RD at A.18.a & A.2.c	
			'A' Coy on Right, 'D' Right Centre, 'C' Coy Left Centre, 'B' Coy Left.	
			at 8.45 pm. Right Coy was strongly attacked by enemy cavalry & infantry & being outflanked was forced to withdraw with severe losses. after sharp hand-to-hand	

2353 Wt. W2544/1454 700,000 5/15 D. D. & L. A.D.S.S./Forms/C. 2118.

Army Form C. 2118.

Instructions regarding War Diaries and Intelligence Summaries are contained in F. S. Regs., Part II. and the Staff Manual respectively. Title pages will be prepared in manuscript.

WAR DIARY
or
INTELLIGENCE SUMMARY.
(Erase heading not required.)

Place	Date	Hour	Summary of Events and Information	Remarks and references to Appendices
BOIS FAVIERE near MARICOURT	24/3/18	11.15pm	At 11.15 pm the outpost line was re-adjusted & was withdrawn to line of E part of BOIS FAVIERE & MARICOURT Rd — ~~[illegible]~~ Major Dixon with Battn. details went to fill gap on left flank of Divl. front near TRONES WOOD	
— do —	25/3/18	am	At 8 a.m. enemy attacked B & C Coys. he made little progress except on ~~right~~ — but Lt. Col Anderson immediately led counter-attack — capturing 70 prisoners & 12 MGs at 11.30 a.m. the whole Divl. front was strongly attacked by the enemy in overwhelming numbers — This battalion was the last to retire & was forced to do so owing to the enemy being around its flanks — the units on each flank having retired — The right (A Coy) did not retire until 20 minutes after its supports & flanks & accounted for hundreds of the enemy. The battalion retired to line of the BOIS MARICOURT but owing to great number of men of ~~all~~ numerous units who had become detached — it was divided up for some time into 3 parties — one under Lt. Col Anderson — another under Major Dixon & the third under Major Cox. The battalion was reorganised by the C.O. and counterattacked at 4.30 pm — One party of the battn. to which was attached about 150	

2353 Wt. W2544/1454 700,000 5/15 D. D. & L. A.D.S.S./Forms/C. 2118.

Instructions regarding War Diaries and Intelligence Summaries are contained in F. S. Regs., Part II. and the Staff Manual respectively. Title pages will be prepared in manuscript.

WAR DIARY
or
INTELLIGENCE SUMMARY.

(*Erase heading not required.*)

Army Form C. 2118.

Place	Date	Hour	Summary of Events and Information	Remarks and references to Appendices
MARICOURT ~~25/3/19~~	25/3/18	—	by Col Anderson was placed, under command of Major J. A. Cox, & attacked on left of battalion. ~~The major part of the battalion was relieved at~~ The counter attack was very successful & cleared the enemy several thousand yards E of MARICOURT & all gains held. Lt Col Anderson & 3 Coy commanders were killed this day. Major Dixon became C.O. The majority of the battalion was relieved at 8 p.m. & proceeded to TALUS WOOD & became, under Capt. TAYLOR the Brigade Rear Guard.	
— —	26/3/18		Major Dixon's party withdrew at 3 a.m. and Major Cox's party at 3.30 a.m. from MARICOURT under orders from 104 Inf Bde — to line BRAY — Major Dixon then got together 4 officers & 120 O.R. of the battalion and under orders of 105 Inf. Bde. gallantly fought the enemy all the next day back to MORLANCOURT — and later covered the whole Div'l retirement right back to BUIRE after severe fighting — Major Cox collected small detached parties at MORLANCOURT during the ~~day~~ & sent them forward, and afterwards proceeded under orders of 106 Inf. Bde. to BUIRE to reconnoitre the defensive position to be occupied that night by the Bn. — He collected all Bn stragglers & occupied the position until Major Dixon & the Rear Guard arrived	

2353 Wt. W2544/1454 700,000 5/15 D. D. & L. A.D.S.S./Forms/C. 2118.

Instructions regarding War Diaries and Intelligence Summaries are contained in F. S. Regs., Part II. and the Staff Manual respectively. Title pages will be prepared in manuscript.

WAR DIARY
or
INTELLIGENCE SUMMARY.
(Erase heading not required.)

Army Form C. 2118.

Place	Date	Hour	Summary of Events and Information	Remarks and references to Appendices
nr BUIRE	26/3/18	10pm	The battalion was re-organised by Major Dixon – and received orders at midnight to proceed to LAVIEVILLE.	
LAVIEVILLE	27/3/18	–	Battalion arrived LAVIEVILLE at 1 a.m. At 12.30 pm orders were received to relieve a Bn of 105 INF BDE at BUIRE – but information came in that enemy was in BUIRE ...	Line 10 "D 19 d" should it is thought read "E 19 d". "Ville sur Corbie" should read Ville sur ANCRE [signature] 14.5.27.
BUIRE			ordered to attack & drive him out & regain river crossings of the [illegible] in that vicinity – It was found en-route that this information was incorrect so relief of SHERWOOD FORESTERS & CHESHIRES was continued. – Relief complete at 4-30pm – The position was from destroyed bridge across the ANCRE on BUIRE – VILLE SUR CORBIE RD to point on AMIENS – ALBERT Rly at about D. 19. d. Patrols were out during the night –	
BUIRE	28/3/18		During the morning the village & our positions were very heavily bombarded & parties of the enemy were observed moving from VILLE towards the ANCRE. These were engaged by our snipers & L.G.s & several casualties to enemy were caused – No attack developed & our casualties were light.	

Army Form C. 2118.

Instructions regarding War Diaries and Intelligence Summaries are contained in F. S. Regs., Part II. and the Staff Manual respectively. Title pages will be prepared in manuscript.

WAR DIARY
or
INTELLIGENCE SUMMARY.
(Erase heading not required.)

Place	Date	Hour	Summary of Events and Information	Remarks and references to Appendices
near BUIRE	26/3/18	10pm	The battalion was re-organised by Major Dixon – and received orders at midnight to proceed to LAVIEVILLE.	
LAVIEVILLE	27/3/18	–	Battalion arrived LAVIEVILLE at 1 a.m. at 12.30 pm orders were received to relieve a Bn of 105 INF BDE on left of BUIRE – but information came in that enemy was in BUIRE & we were	
BUIRE			ordered to attack & drive him out & regain river crossings of ~~the~~ R. ANCRE in that vicinity – It was found en-route that this information was incorrect so relief of SHERWOOD FORESTERS & CHESHIRES was continued. – Relief complete at 4.30pm – The position was from destroyed bridge across the ANCRE on BUIRE – VILLE sur CORBIE RD to point on AMIENS – ALBERT RLWY at about D.19.d. Patrols were out during the night –	
BUIRE	28/3/18		During the morning the village & our positions were very heavily bombarded & parties of the enemy were observed moving from VILLE towards the ANCRE. These were engaged by our snipers & L.G.s & several casualties to enemy were caused – No attack developed & our casualties were light.	

Instructions regarding War Diaries and Intelligence Summaries are contained in F. S. Regs., Part II. and the Staff Manual respectively. Title pages will be prepared in manuscript.

WAR DIARY

or

~~INTELLIGENCE~~ SUMMARY.

(Erase heading not required.)

Army Form C. 2118.

Place	Date	Hour	Summary of Events and Information	Remarks and references to Appendices
BUIRE	29/3/19	–	Battalion relieved by 19th L.F. Day passed quietly and Bn. proceeded to support position on road in D 24 c.	
Nr. BUIRE	30/3/19	–	Battalion still in support – Day passed quietly	
		8 pm	Battn proceeded to LA NEUVILLE to billets	
LA NEUVILLE	"	10-30 pm	Battn billeted at LA NEUVILLE	
— do —	31/3/19	—	——— do – Battn marched from LA NEUVILLE to billets at HEILLY at 7 pm.	
		9 pm	Battn arrived and billeted at HEILLY	

[signature] Major
for OC 12th H.L.I.

2353 Wt. W2544/1454 700,000 5/15 D. D. & L. A.D.S.S./Forms/C. 2118.

12th Battalion Highland Light Infantry

NARRATIVE OF OPERATIONS - 23/3/18 to 30/3/18.

Ref. Map Sheets - 57c, 62c and 62 d, 1/40,000.

Saturday 23rd Mch. 1918 — The Battalion (less one Company) marched out of "J" Camp, PESELHOEK at 5.30 a.m. to PROVEN where it entrained at 9 a.m., detraining at HEILLY at 10.30 p.m. "D" Company entrained at the same place at 3 p.m. The Battalion strength was 32 Officers, 830 O.R. and commanded by Lieut. Col. W.H. ANDERSON.

On reaching HEILLY orders were received to proceed to billets at BRAY-sur-Somme.

Sunday 24th March 1918 — The Battalion arrived there at 3.20 a.m. tired after long journey and march. Orders were then received to be prepared to move at any moment, and the Battalion were equipped in fighting order, being completed with S.A.A. and Bombs, and rations being issued. Orders were then received to proceed to MARICOURT where the Division were concentrating. At 7.30 a.m. the Battalion (less one Company) proceeded with Advance Guard to MARICOURT where it was halted about 9 a.m. At midday, orders were received that the Battalion (less one Company) was attached to the 9th Division, and had to proceed to HARDECOURT-aux-Bois, and take up a defensive position astride the village. That was accomplished by 2 p.m. At 2.15 p.m. orders were received to attack and occupy MMAREPAS and ridge N.E. of it. This was successfully done "B" Company under Capt. Johnstone attacking on right - "C" Company under Capt. Graeme Taylor on the left with "A" Company in support.

No British troops could be found on either flank, and orders were shortly afterwards received to evacuate the ~~xx~~ position and re-occupy HARDECOURT Ridge. Here also it was found impossible to gain touch with any units on the flanks. At 5 p.m. "D" Company joined the Battalion having detrained at HEILLY and marched thence via BRAY and MARICOURT. At 7 p.m. orders were received to withdraw to an outpost line astride the HARDECOURT-MARICOURT Road about A.18.a. and A.12.c. This was done, dispositions being -"A" Company - Right, "D" Company - Right Centre, "C" Company - Left Centre, and "B" Company on Left. Touch was here gained with a unit of the 30th Division on the Right. At 8.45 p.m. our Right Company was attacked, the enemy getting round the flank, and after sharp hand-to-hand fighting were forced to a position on high ground astride the Road in A.17.b. Towards mid-night the line was re-adjusted so as to conform with position of troops on flanks, and a new line taken up on ridge in BOIS FAVIERE, with posts pushed forward into the valley. This entailed a slight alteration of dispositions, and "B" Company was moved from the left and put in Right Centre between "A" Company and "D" Company. The Battalion was now in touch with a Company of the 9th Divisional Details on the Left. The strength of the Battalion taken into action was 27 Officers 693 O.R. Transport and Details remained West of MARICOURT, moving at 8 p.m. to Brigade Hqrs. in Ravine West of TALUS BOIS (A.9.c.)

Monday/

Monday 25th March 1918

At 3 a.m. I was informed by Brigade that Lieut. Col. Anderson was missing and that a gap existed in line between THRONES WOOD and BOIS FAVIERE, and was ordered to proceed there with Details and 20 men of 106th T.M.Battery under Lieut. Laing, to fill gap, then to find and take over command of the Battalion.

At 4 a.m. I proceeded with Details 12th H.L.I. - strength 4 Officers and 40 O.R. and detachment of 106th T.M.B., and took up position in A.5.a. and S.29.d. at dawn. I then proceeded to join Battalion with 1 Officer. That position was attacked unsuccessfully twice during the morning, but they were eventually forced to retire on to the BRI UETORIE, where all the officers having become casualties, they attached themselves to the 18th H.L.I.

Lieut. Col. Anderson was found to be still commanding the Battalion at BOIS FAVIERE.

8 a.m. About 8 a.m. the enemy delivered a strong attack which broke down on the left, but was temporarily successful on the right where he got into the wood and penetrated as far as A.11.d.1.6. Lieut. Col. Anderson immediately organised and led a counter-attack which restored the situation, and 70 prisoners with 12 machine guns were captured.

About 11 a.m. an attack again developed, the enemy advancing in great numbers.

At 12 noon the left Company reported that the troops on left had retired and that the enemy had passed his left flank and were on high ground in rear. They had also got through on the right, and Lieut. Col. Anderson ordered the withdrawal to commence to a line of trenches N.E. of MERICOURT, held by Engineers. This was successfully done, but the right Company got detached and took up a position in the South of BOIS de MARICOURT. Later, the Battalion was forced to withdraw through the BOIS de MARICOURT and was re-organised by Lieut. Col. Anderson on road North of MARICOURT in A.16.a.

MARICOURT

At 4.30 p.m. in conjunction with the D.L.I. on left and various Details including 17th Entrenching Battalion on right, he counter-attacked, driving the enemy from the wood-yard and northern portion of BOIS de MARICOURT which was consolidated. The enemy, suffering severe casualties, retired over Ridge at BOIS FAVIERE.

Lieut. Col. Anderson was killed here, and I took over command, but was only able to get some 60 men of the Battalion organised under my command.

The Battalion was now divided in two main portions, the left half in the Northern portion of BOIS de MARICOURT, and the right half, 5 Officers and 135 men under Lieut. Sillars in the S.E. of MARICOURT. The latter party, right half Battalion, was relieved here at 8 p.m. and ordered to proceed to Brigade Headquarters at TALUS Wood. This it did, and Capt. Grahame Taylor there joined them and took over command. On orders, an outpost position was taken up East of TALUS Wood to cover the withdrawal of the Brigade. The Left half Battalion though keeping in touch with Brigade Headquarters by orderly, received no orders.

The Transport moved to BRAY in the morning where it remained.

Tuesday./

Tuesday 26th March 1918

The Right Half Battalion remained on outpost till receiving orders to with-draw at 3 a.m., which it did, proceeding with Rear Guard by the MARICOURT-CARNOY-FRICOURT-MEAULTE-MORLANCOURT Road at 7 a.m. When within 1 kilo of MORLANCOURT orders were received to await the arrival of the Brigade. About 8 a.m. orders were received to proceed by the Railway to the ALBERT-BRAY Road where it took up an outpost position to the North of the Railway, being in touch with 105th Infantry Brigade on Right and 18th H.L.I. on Left. The Left Half Battalion received orders about 1.45 a.m. from 104th Infantry Brigade to withdraw to the BRAY-ALBERT Road. This was done, and touch was gained with Headquarters, 105th Brigade who could give no information as to the position of the 106th Infantry Brigade, and ordered me to remain with them. I had now 4 Officers and 120 O.R. under my command.

At 8 a.m. touch was gained with Colonel Lawrenson, commanding 106th Infantry Brigade, and orders received to proceed to MORLANCOURT and await orders. It was reached at 12 noon when General Pollard ordered me to take up a position covering MORLANCOURT. This I proceeded to do, and Colonel Lawrenson later gave me verbal orders to cover the withdrawal of the Division through MORLANCOURT, but not, if possible, to become seriously engaged with the enemy, after which a written order was received that after the evacuation of MORLANCOURT had been covered, a position was to be taken up on high ground at J.6.c. near MARETT Wood, covering the crossing of the ANCRE at TREUX, and then send to the Church at VILLE-sur-ANCRE for orders.

A positoon was consolidated on the plateau East of MORLANCOURT astride the road from there to the Northern portion of the BOIS des TAILLES (about K.10.b.3.3.)

Meanwhile the Right Half Battalion having no orders, conformed to the movements of the troops on either flank, and withdrew slowly through MORLANCOURT to the North of the River ANCRE, where they received orders to occupy Sunken Road, 800 yards North of BUIRE sur l'ANCRE.

The Left Half Battalion in a short time had dug excellent cover with entrenching tools, and at 2.30 p.m. troops began passing through them.

By 4 p.m. all formed bodies had passed through, but stretcher parties continued till 4.45 p.m. From 4 p.m. the position was subjected to severe bombardment, and the cover dug earlier proved invaluable, few casualties being sustained. The enemy was engaged with Lewis Guns and Snipers, until within about 500 yards which was about 5 p.m. The withdrawal was then commenced and the Battalion concentrated West of MORLANCOURT, marching thence in Artillery Formation across country to MARETT Wood. A post of 1 Officer and 20 men was established astride the SAILLY le SEC to VILLE sur ANCRE Road about K.7.b. until dark when it was withdrawn.

With the remainder I took up a position on high ground at North East of MARETT Wood covering all approaches to TREUX and VILLE sur ANCRE with Lewis Gun Posts, and covered the withdrawal of all troops over the ANCRE, which was complete before dark about 7.30 p.m.

My/

My Adjutant proceeded to VILLE sur ANCRE for orders. He reported at 9 p.m. that he could get in touch with no- and that thelast troops had passed through the village shortly after 8 p.m., so knowing that the orders for the Division were to take up a position North of the ANCRE, and having completed my duties in covering the withdrawal, and fearing the enemy might cut me off in the dark, I decided to withdraw, and I crossed the River about 10 p.m. and then proceeded to join the remainder of the Battalion who I was told were in Sunken Road West of BUIRE. There the Battalion was re-organised, and later, on orders from Brigade, proceeded to billets in LAVIEVILLE where it arrived about 1 a.m. on the 28th March.

Wednesday 27th March 1918

At 12.30 p.m. received orders to relieve Sherwood Foresters and Details of the Cheshires in Sector BUIRE sur ANCRE - VILLE sur ANCRE Road inclusive to point on Railway 1000 yards from Station about D.19.d.6.0. After the orders had been issued, information came in that the enemy had attacked and occupied the village of BUIRE. The Battalion was ordered to counter-attack and re-established the situation by re-gaining the crossings of the ANCRE at BUIRE. This the Battalion proceeded to do and advanced in Artillery Formation, "B" Company on Right, "A" Company on Left, "C" Company in Support to Right, "D" Company in Support to Left.
The 17th Battalion, Royal Scots advanced on the Left. A few casualties were suffered in crossing the ALBERT-AMIENS Road. On reaching the BUIRE sur ANCRE Cemetry, the Officer i/c 35th Divisional Details in position there, informed me that the position was still intact, so the relief of the Sherwoods was continued, relief being complete by 4.30 p.m.
Dispositions were - "A" Company on Right astride the BUIRE sur ANCRE - VILLE sur ANCRE Road with posts guarding bridge which was partially destroyed and had charge lodged ready to demolish it if found necessary, -"C" Company Centre along railway bank, - "D" Company Left and "B" Company in Support in uarry North of Station. The 104th Infantry Brigade were in touch on the Right, and the 17th Royal Scots on the Left. The day passed quietly. Patrols were sent out along the river banks at dusk remaining out all night, and forward posts were established.

Thursday 28th March 1918

Very quiet at Stand To, but during the morning occasional heavy bombardments of positions and village, increasing in intensity till between 5 p.m. and 6 p.m. From 10 a.m. onwards enemy observed moving West to VILLE sur ANCRE, and during afternoon, moving forward towards the ANCRE. This movement was engaged by Lewis Guns and Snipers and many hits obtained. It was expected an attack might develop but nothing occurred, and the night passed quietly, -The usual Patrol Posts being pushed out.
"B" Company relieved "A" Company on the Right.

Friday/

Friday 29th March 1918 — The day passed quietly. The 19th L.F. relieved the Battalion at night, relief being complete by 9.30 p.m. The Battalion proceeded to Divisional Reserve in Sunken Road in D.24.c.

Saturday 30th March 1918 — The day passed quietly, and at 8 p.m. the Division having been relieved, the Battalion proceeded to billets at LA NEUVILLE

Major
2/4/18 — Comdg. 12th Battn. Highland L.I.

APPENDIX "A"

ROLL OF OFFICER CASUALTIES

Major W. H. Anderson	Killed	25/3/18
Capt. R.M.Johnstone	do	do
Capt. R.L.Hannah	do	do
Lieut. H. Stewart	do	do
Lieut. E. H. Winch	do	do
2nd Lieut. J. Brown	do	26/3/18
Lieut. I. W. Hardie	Wounded	25/3/18
2nd Lieut. C. Neil	do	25/3/18
2nd Lieut. W. Dunlop	do	do
2nd Lieut. E. Noble	do	do
Lieut. (A/Capt) G. Taylor	do	26/3/18
2nd Lieut. W. McKenzie	do	27/3/18
Lieut. A. L. Bryson	do	25/3/18
2nd Lieut. J. Callan	do	25/3/18
Lieut. J. Hunter	Missing	25/3/18
2nd Lieut. J. Forsyth	Died of Wounds	28/3/18

APPENDIX "B"

TOTAL CASUALTIES - OTHER RANKS

Killed -	33
Wounded -	183
Missing -	110
Total	326

WAR
DIARY

A

12th Battalion Highland Light Infantry

SECRET ORDERS BY MAJOR W. H. ANDERSON 6th March 1918

Ref. Map St. Julien, 1/10,000
and Belgium 20 S.E. and S.W.

1. The 106th Infantry Brigade will relieve the 104th Infantry Brigade in the line on the night 7/8th inst.

2. The 12th H.L.I. will relieve the 18th L.F. in the Right Sub-Sector of the Brigade Front.

3. (a) Dispositions of Companies in the line will be as follows:-

"B" Company.	-	Right Front
"C" do	-	Left Front
"A" do	-	Support
"D" do	-	Reserve

(b) Companies of 12th H.L.I. will relieve Companies of 18th L.F. as follows:-

"B" Coy.-12th	H.L.I.	will relieve	"Z" Coy.	18th L.F.
"C" "	"	"	"Y" "	"
"A" "	"	"	"X" "	"
"D" "	"	"	"W" "	"

4. A train to convey the two Front Line Companies, Support Company and Headquarters Company will leave ELVERDINGHE Station at 12.30 p.m.
Detrain at KEMPTON PARK.
Reserve Company will proceed by march route.

5. PARADE.
(a) All Companies will parade 100 strong, but the Companies proceeding to the Front Line will detach 20 O.R. each, to be accommodated in EAGLE TRENCH under the command of O.C. Reserve Company.
These will be available for Working Parties under Battalion arrangements.

(b) "B", "C" "A" and Hqrs. Companies will parade at 12 noon on Football Field in Fighting Order - Water Bottle full - and, proceeding to ELVERDINGHE Station, will entrain at 12.30 p.m. for KEMPTON PARK Station, thence to PIG and WHISTLE by march route.
"D" Company will parade at 3.45 p.m. under the orders of Capt. Hannah, and move to the line by march route, - Cross Roads, B.10.d.5.6. - BOESINGHE - PIG and WHISTLE, and to be clear of LARRY Camp by 4 p.m.

6. GUIDES will be at PIG and WHISTLE at 4.30 p.m.
"Post" Guides for Front Line Companies will meet Companies on the respective duck-board tracks in vicinity of Company Hqrs. as previously.

7. RATIONS.
Each man of "B", "C", "A" and Hqrs. Companies will be in possession of two days rations before moving off.
Rations for "D" Company will be put in sand-bags, labelled, and dumped beside Officers' Mess Gear going into the line.
The Quarter Master will arrange to send up to the Cook-house at EAGLE DUMP 10 Camp Kettles.
The Sergeant Cook will supervise all cooking and the issue of water, and the loading of the petrol tins on the limber for

7. RATIONS. contd.
for transport to the Stores.

8. WATER.
70 tins of water will be conveyed by limber, and will be issued at EAGLE DUMP to Companies as under:-

"B"	Company.	-	12
"C"	do	-	12
"A"	do	-	12
"D"	do	-	12
Hqrs.	do	-	8

This is a 24 hours supply of drinking water.
The remainder of the water will be conveyed by Company Cooks to Cook-house and used for cooking purposes.
These petrol tins must be returned to the Sergeant Cook at the Cook-house by 6.30 p.m. if a nightly supply of water is to be maintained.

9. TOMMY COOKERS.
The Quarter Master will issue with rations tomorrow, for use in the line during the 1st 48 hours, the following number of Tommy Cookers:-

"B" and "C" Companies	-	50 each.
"A" Company	-	20.

A Regimental Reserve of 30 tins, in addition to above, will be sent by limber, and so labelled, to EAGLE DUMP, whence they will be conveyed to Battalion Headquarters.

10. BLANKETS and PACKS.
(a) Blankets of men proceeding to the line will be rolled in bundles of ten, labelled and stacked in "A" Company's lines near Water Point by 9 a.m.
Packs at the same place by 9.30 a.m.
(b) Blankets of men remaining with Details will be stacked in a similar fashion, at a point nearby, under the Quarter Master's orders by 12 noon.

11. VALISES.
Officers' Valises will be collected alongside "10(b)" by 10.30 a.m.

12. MESS GEAR, ORDERLY ROOM STORES ETC.
(a) For the Line. - On road near Headquarters Mess. 12 noon
(b) For Details. - With Officers' Valises. 1 pm

13. ADVANCE PARTY.
One N.C.O. per Company will proceed to the line to-night to take over Trench Stores etc.

14. REAR PARTY.
A Rear Party will be supplied by Details to clean up and hand over LARRY Camp. Lieut. Stewart will hand over and obtain a certificate that the Camp has been left in a clean and sanitary condition.

15./

Instructions regarding War Diaries and Intelligence Summaries are contained in F. S. Regs., Part II. and the Staff Manual respectively. Title pages will be prepared in manuscript.

WAR DIARY
or
~~INTELLIGENCE SUMMARY.~~
(Erase heading not required.)

12th Bn. Highland L. I.

Army Form C. 2118.

1–30 April 1918

Vol 29

R 1

Place	Date	Hour	Summary of Events and Information	Remarks and references to Appendices
HEILLY	1918 Apl. 1		Battalion in Billets in HEILLY & engaged in cleaning up & re-organising.	
	2		Battalion in Billets as above. Weather dry but cold. Continuation of reorganisation & refitting. Company Commanders reconnoitre new area of defence to the EAST of the village.	
	3		Battalion in Billets as above. Weather very wet & proposed short route march cancelled. Brigade warned to be prepared to move on half hours notice.	
	4		Battalion in Billets as above	
	5		do Weather dry. About 6-50 p.m. orders received to move with Packs & blankets. At 8 p.m. the Battalion move to FRANKVILLERS where packs & blankets are stored & the men equip themselves in Fighting Order. A move to a position 3 Kilometres EAST of the village is made to a position NORTH of the main ALBERT–AMIENS road, where the Battalion is in reserve to an Australian Division.	

A5834 Wt. W4973/M687 750,000 8/16 D. D. & L. Ltd. Forms/C.2118/13.

29. M
16 sheets

Instructions regarding War Diaries and Intelligence Summaries are contained in F. S. Regs., Part II. and the Staff Manual respectively. Title pages will be prepared in manuscript.

WAR DIARY
or
INTELLIGENCE SUMMARY.
(Erase heading not required.)

Army Form C. 2118.

R.2

Place	Date	Hour	Summary of Events and Information	Remarks and references to Appendices
IN THE LINE	1918 APL 6		The Battalion occupy a disused system of trenches ~~into~~ which they find after much difficulty owing to the darkness of the night, & to there being no guides. Trenches are very wet & afford very little cover & consequently the men spend a very miserable night. Head Quarters occupy a very da[mp] & broken-down dug-out in the trench-system. The Battalion is in position by about 2.30 A.M. & at dawn the positions of Companies are re-adjusted where necessary. At noon orders are received to proceed to FRANKVILLERS & collect packs & blankets. On arrival the men are issued with a hot meal & rest in the village. C.O. rides on to WARLOY for orders, returning about 5.30 p.m. with instructions that the Battalion proceed to take over the LINE at AVELUY WOOD from the 24th London Regiment. March is continued amidst a downpour of rain, VIA WARLOY, HEDAUVILLE, ENGLEBELMER, & MARTINSART, arriving in the line	

A5834 Wt. W4973/M687 750,000 8/16 D. D. & L. Ltd. Forms/C.2118/13

Army Form C. 2118.

Instructions regarding War Diaries and Intelligence Summaries are contained in F. S. Regs., Part II. and the Staff Manual respectively. Title pages will be prepared in manuscript.

WAR DIARY
or
INTELLIGENCE SUMMARY.
(Erase heading not required.)

Place	Date	Hour	Summary of Events and Information	Remarks and references to Appendices
	1918			
IN THE LINE	APL. 7		shortly after midnight. Men utterly exhausted & very miserable. Relief completed by 3.15 A.M. with no casualties. LINE consists of isolated posts in the wood. Disposition of Companies is as under RIGHT "C", CENTRE "B" LEFT "A", SUPPORT "D".	
			Morning passed without incident. Still very wet & men complaining of their feet & general condition of misery. Ration parties coming through MARTINSART are shelled, but have no casualties.	
	8		Night passed quietly. From 5.45 to 6.30 A.M. valley between village & the wood heavily strafed also the village sides & some of the posts. otherwise the day passed without incident. The sniper exceedingly active during the day. Enemy movement on LEFT Company front engaged with L.G. fire. During afternoon & evening posts of LEFT HALF of "R" Coy advanced 50 yards & two new posts established. During the night a certain amount of wiring is done. Night again very wet & dark & much difficulty experienced in getting round the posts in the wood. 2/Lieut. J. BAUCHOP wounded.	

Instructions regarding War Diaries and Intelligence Summaries are contained in F. S. Regs., Part II. and the Staff Manual respectively. Title pages will be prepared in manuscript.

WAR DIARY
or
INTELLIGENCE SUMMARY.
(Erase heading not required.)

Army Form C. 2118.

R 4

Place	Date	Hour	Summary of Events and Information	Remarks and references to Appendices
IN THE LINE	1918 APL 9		Night passed quietly. At 5.30 AM. heavy bombardment of path, edge of wood & valley, continuing till 9 A.M. no infantry action following on our front, but small attack on LEFT of Batt. on our R. Dry weather now with considerable warmth enabling the men to get dry.	
			Day passes quietly on the whole. Between 2.30 & 5.30 pm an enemy plane flew over our lines at a low altitude & fired a Machine Gun at our front line Posts. About 5.30 pm. enemy tried to rush LEFT Coy. Lewis Gun Post. Three men wounded by bombs but enemy driven back into thicket, one man being badly wounded in the back as he disappeared.	
			Work during the night consisted of wiring posts & improving trenches. The village of MARTINSART & adjoining valley strafed between 11.30 p.m. & 1.30 A.M. Draft of 196 O.R. received.	
	10		Night passed quietly otherwise. Stand-to very quiet. Our snipers very active, & secure many hits.	

A5834 Wt. W4973/M687 750,000 8/16 D. D. & L. Ltd. Forms/C.2118/13

Instructions regarding War Diaries and Intelligence Summaries are contained in F. S. Regs., Part II. and the Staff Manual respectively. Title pages will be prepared in manuscript.

WAR DIARY
or
INTELLIGENCE SUMMARY.
(Erase heading not required.)

Army Form C. 2118.

R 5

Place	Date	Hour	Summary of Events and Information	Remarks and references to Appendices
	1918			
IN THE LINE	Apl. 10		Between 9.30 & 11 A.M. enemy aeroplane flew over RIGHT Coys area at a height of 100 feet & later in the day the enemy opened with 5.9's & 4.2's & light T.M.s on our front line posts securing several direct hits on posts. Medium T.M.s were fired on LEFT Coys' area & enemy M.G.s opened when they burst in the hope of catching movement. Much Machine Gun Activity in the evening. Very dark night. Wiring continued. Draft of 40 O.R. received	
	11		Corps expect attack but night & stand-to in the morning pass quietly. MARTINSART & valley EAST of village shelled between 5 & 5.30 A.M., but otherwise day passed quietly. Village again shelled between 5 & 5.30 p.m. & during evening.	
			Battalion relieved by 17th Lancashire Fusiliers. Relief complete by 11.5 p.m. Companies march back to billets in HEDAUVILLE	
HEDAUVILLE	12		arriving about 3.15 A.M. Stood-to at 4.45 A.M. till 5.45. Remainder of day spent in resting & cleaning up. C.O. & Company Commrs reconnoitred Battle Positions. Draft of 31 O.R. received. Casualties for the tour 3 killed & 16 wounded.	

A5834 Wt. W4973/M687 750,000 8/16 D. D. & L. Ltd. Forms/C.2118/13

Instructions regarding War Diaries and Intelligence Summaries are contained in F. S. Regs., Part II. and the Staff Manual respectively. Title pages will be prepared in manuscript.

WAR DIARY
or
INTELLIGENCE SUMMARY.
(Erase heading not required.)

Army Form C. 2118.

R.L.

Place	Date	Hour	Summary of Events and Information	Remarks and references to Appendices
	1919			
HEDAUVILLE	APL 13		Battalion in Billets in HEDAUVILLE. Stood to from 4.45 – 5.45 A.M. Day spent in refitting & re-organising. Draft of 38 O.R. received.	
	14		Battalion in Billets in Hedauville. Slight shelling of the village by H.V. shells but no casualties. Weather dry & cold. The Battalion moves from HEDAUVILLE into Brigade Reserve in BOUZINCOURT with H.Qrs. in cellar in the village & the Companies accomodated in a Sunken Road 200 yards to the NORTH of it. Relief complete by 10.30 p.m.	
IN THE LINE	15		Battalion in Brigade Reserve as above. BOUZINCOURT shelled during the day. No casualties. Men engaged in salvage. Slight aerial activity on the part of the enemy for observation purposes.	
	16		Battalion in reserve as above. Village shelled during the day & at Stand-To otherwise the day passed without incident. Draft of 21 O.R. received by Details at WARLOY	

A5834 Wt. W4973/M687 750,000 8/16 D. D. & L. Ltd. Forms/C.2118/13

Instructions regarding War Diaries and Intelligence Summaries are contained in F. S. Regs., Part II. and the Staff Manual respectively. Title pages will be prepared in manuscript.

WAR DIARY
or
INTELLIGENCE SUMMARY.
(Erase heading not required.)

Army Form C. 2118.

R7

Place	Date	Hour	Summary of Events and Information	Remarks and references to Appendices
	1918			
IN THE LINE	APL. 16		The Battalion move into the LINE from Brigade Reserve taking over from the 17th Royal Scots in the RIGHT SUB-SECTION of the RIGHT SUB-SECTOR of the Divisional Front. Relief complete by 12 midnight	
	17		Night passes without incident. Considerable artillery activity but principally on back areas. During the day the village is shelled by 5.9.s A report is received that during relief the previous night the enemy sent over a number of gas shells in the vicinity of "A" Coy by which 14 men were gassed & had to be evacuated.	
			Companies' Dispositions in the LINE are:- RIGHT "B" Coy. LEFT "D" Company, IMM. SUPPORT "A" Coy. MAIN SUPPORT "C" Coy.	
	18		Battalion in the Line as above.	
			LT-COL. J. N. O. RYECROFT, D.S.O. M.C. assumes command of the Battalion.	
			Artillery active at Stand-To, but no infantry action develops. Enemy Aircraft flies low over our Front Line.	

Instructions regarding War Diaries and Intelligence Summaries are contained in F. S. Regs., Part II. and the Staff Manual respectively. Title pages will be prepared in manuscript.

WAR DIARY
or
INTELLIGENCE SUMMARY.
(Erase heading not required.)

Army Form C. 2118.

R.8

Place	Date	Hour	Summary of Events and Information	Remarks and references to Appendices
IN THE LINE	1918 APL 19		Battalion in the Line. Weather dry & cold. Stand-To quiet with some Artillery activity. During the night considerable Wiring done by the various Companies. Front Line trenches deepened & drained, & supplies to ammunition & bombs brought from Brigade Dump to make up Company Dumps in the Front Line.	
	20		Battalion in the Line. Artillery activity continues, but day passes without incident.	
			Draft of the following 14 Officers received from the Base.	
			Capt. R. CRICHTON, Capt. J. HOUSTON, LIEUT. C. L. SCOTT, LIEUT. A. ANDERSON, LIEUT A. McDOUGALL, LIEUT. M.H. LAUGHLAND, LIEUT. H. C. JONAS, LIEUT. R. S. BROWN, LIEUT. H. J. STANFORD, LIEUT. W. D. RONALD, LIEUT. M. L. BURNET, LIEUT. J. A. ROBERTSON, LIEUT. A. C. TODD, LIEUT. N. M. CLARK.	
			The Battalion is relieved by the 17th Lancashire Fusiliers & moves into Brigade Reserve, & is accomodated in Cubby Holes & tents in valley 1000 YDS. EAST of HEDAUVILLE.	
			Total Casualties of this Tour 5 killed & 24 wounded.	

A5834 Wt. W4973/M687 750,000 8/16 D. D. & L. Ltd. Forms/C.2118/13

Instructions regarding War Diaries and Intelligence Summaries are contained in F. S. Regs., Part II. and the Staff Manual respectively. Title pages will be prepared in manuscript.

WAR DIARY
or
INTELLIGENCE SUMMARY.
(*Erase heading not required.*)

Army Form C. 2118.

R 9

Place	Date	Hour	Summary of Events and Information	Remarks and references to Appendices
HEDAUVILLE	1919 APL 21		Relief complete by 12.30 A.M. The Battalion in Brigade Reserve. Men occupied in cleaning up during the day. At 9.30 p.m. an enemy aeroplane flew over camp & dropped two bombs, one of which, dropping in a bivouac, killed two men & wounded one other.	
	22		Battalion in Brigade Reserve. Day passes quietly. LIEUT. H.E. BETHUNE rejoins Battalion.	
	23		do do, LIEUT. J.F. SHIRLAW joins Battalion & 2/LIEUT. H. COWAN rejoins.	
AVELUY WOOD	~~"~~		~~do~~ The Battalion moved into the line, relieving the 18th Bn SHERWOODS in the left sub-section of the Centre Section. Relief complete 11.30 pm. Dispositions - Right - C Coy. Centre - B Coy. - Left A Coy. Support D Coy.	
	24		Night passed quietly. Enemy opened usual bombardment of valley & village at morning "Stand to". Enemy M.Gs active throughout the night on ridge & wood.	
	25		Enemy T.Ms troublesome during the day. Our L Gs active & enemy sniping & M.G. fire considerably reduced in consequence.	
	26		Night & day passed quietly	

A5834 Wt. W4973/M687 750,000 8/16 D. D. & L. Ltd. Forms/C.2118/13

Instructions regarding War Diaries and Intelligence Summaries are contained in F. S. Regs., Part II. and the Staff Manual respectively. Title pages will be prepared in manuscript.

WAR DIARY
or
INTELLIGENCE SUMMARY.
(Erase heading not required.)

Army Form C. 2118.

R.10

Place	Date	Hour	Summary of Events and Information	Remarks and references to Appendices
AVELUY WOOD	27.		Night passed with usual intermittent M.G. fire. Day quiet.	
	28.		At 8.30pm Enemy artillery opened a barrage on his usual lines. TMs & light shells on the WOOD, 5.9s etc on the valley. At 8.43pm enemy attempted to attack Centre Coy, S.O.S was sent up & our barrage opened at 8.45pm. Enemy did not reach our lines & all was quiet again by 9.30pm. The rest of the night was quiet, & the day passed with the usual intermittent Artillery activity.	
	29.		During the morning enemy bombed night posts of right Coy causing a few casualties. Enemy were dispersed & rest of day passed quietly. Battalion was relieved by the 17th Lancs Fus. Relief complete by 1am.	
	30.		Battalion on relief withdrew to V.S.a. without casualties & went into bivouacs. Total casualties during tour Lt. SCOTT wounded, 4 killed, & 34 wounded. Day spent in cleaning up.	

[signature] Lt. Col.
Comdg. 12th High. L. I.

A5834 Wt. W4973/M687 750,000 8/16 D. D. & L. Ltd. Forms/C.2118/13

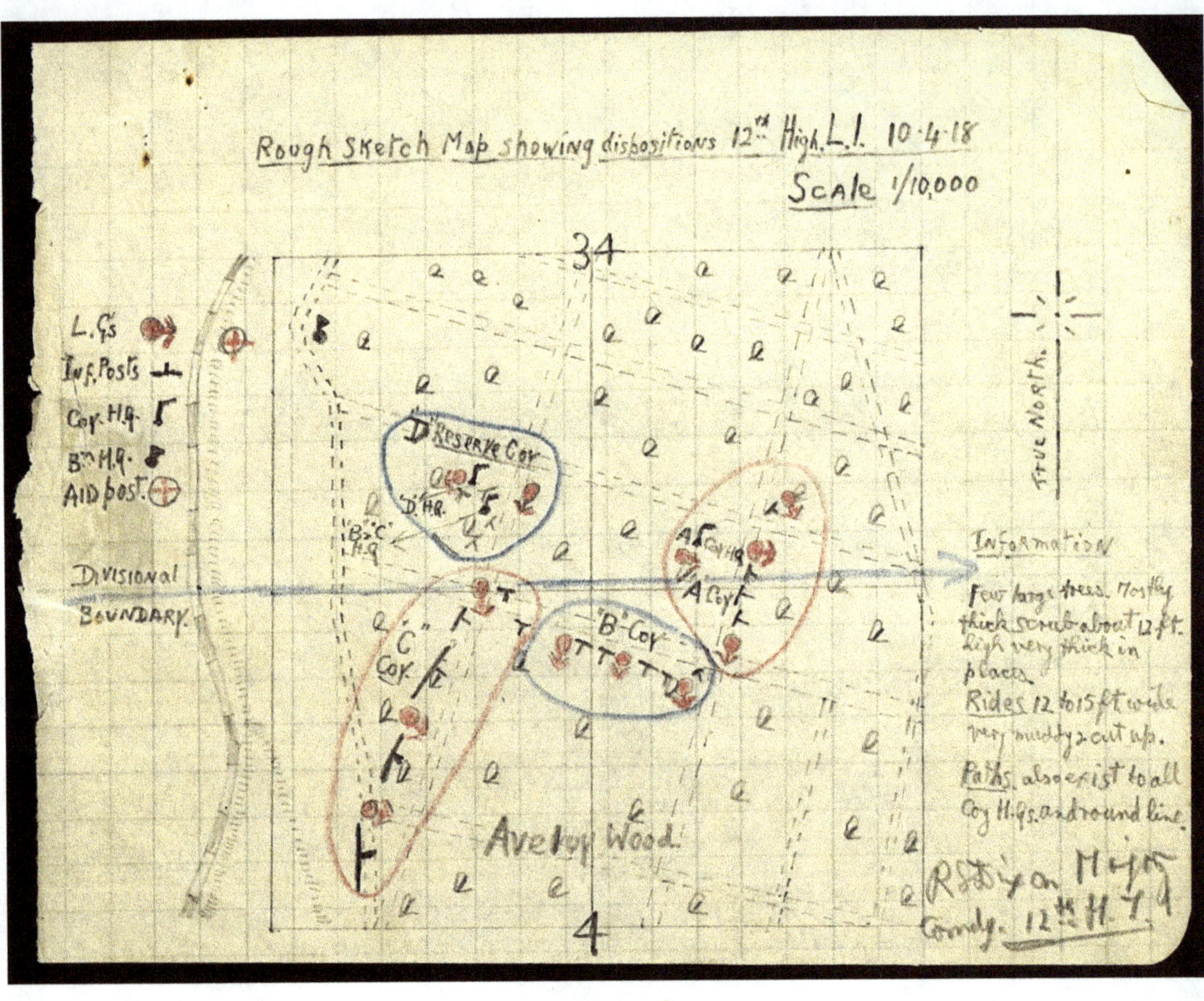

Rough Sketch Map showing dispositions 12th High. L.I. 10.4.18
Scale 1/10,000
34
L.Gs
Inf. Posts
Coy. H.Q.
Bn. H.Q.
Aid post
Divisional Boundary
'D' Reserve Coy
'C' Coy.
'B' Coy
A Coy
Aveluy Wood
4
True North
Information
Few large trees. Mostly thick scrub about 12 ft. high very thick in places.
Rides 12 to 15 ft wide very muddy & cut up.
Paths also exist to all Coy H.Qs. and round line.
R S Dixon Major
Comdg. 12th H.L.I.

/10.

Copy No ....
SECRET

106th [illegible] BRIGADE ORDER NO S., 12.

Ref. Sheet [illegible] S.E.

Action of Brigade in Divisional Reserve in case of attack.

1. On receipt of Code word " OCCUPY " Battalions will move to positions of readiness in the valley as follows:-

12th High.L.I.	V.5.central, & sunken road V.5.c.4.8. - V.5.a.9.3.	
17th R.Scots.	V.5.d.5.8. -	V.6.a.0.4.
18th High.L.I.	V.6.a.0.5. -	P.36.c.5.5.

2. If the Reserve Battalion of the Right Front Brigade is moved forward from the sunken road in W.1.D. and W.7.b. the 12th High.L.I. will move forward and will occupy this sunken road. They will be at the tactical call of the Right front Brigade in case of emergency. O.C. 12th High.L.I. will arrange to get in touch with O.C. Reserve Battalion of Right Front Brigade to ascertain when the Reserve Battalion moves forward.

3. The remainder of the Reserve Brigade will remain in Divisional Reserve in the above mentioned valley and will be prepared to occupy and hold to the last the Corps line in W.7.c. - W.1.b. (ENGLEBELMER - MILLENCOURT LINE) if the enemy should break through the front system.

17th R.Scots. From V.18.b.8.5. - W.1.c.8.0.
18th High.L.I. From W.1.c.8.0. - W.1.a.9.9.

4. If however the situation can be restored by a deliberate counter attack and fresh troops are coming up to hold the Corps line, this Brigade may be thrown into the Counter attack under instructions from 35th Division.

5. 106th T.M.Batt will remain in its present location and will send an Officer to report at Brigade H.Q. on receipt of Code word " OCCUPY "

6. Brigade Units to acknowledge.

Issued at 12. noon.

C. L. [illegible]
Captain,
Brigade Major.
106th Infantry Brigade.

Copy 1 & 2. War Diary
3. O.O.File
4 & 5. 35th Division
6. 17th R.Scots.
7. 12th High.L.I.
8. 18th High.L.I.
9. 106th T.M.Batt
10. 104th Inf. Bde.

Copy 11. 105 Inf. Bde.
12. C.R.A.
13. No 4 Co Train.
14. Signals.
15. Staff Captain.
16. Staff Captain (Rear)
17. G.O.C.

Instructions regarding War Diaries and Intelligence Summaries are contained in F. S. Regs., Part II. and the Staff Manual respectively. Title pages will be prepared in manuscript.

WAR DIARY
or
~~INTELLIGENCE~~ SUMMARY.
(Erase heading not required.)

12th Bn HIGHLAND. L.I

From 1st to 31st May 1918

Army Form C. 2118.

VR 30

Place	Date	Hour	Summary of Events and Information	Remarks and references to Appendices
1918	1917			
RUBEMPRÉ	MAY 1		Battalion in Tented Camp on outskirts of RUBEMPRÉ village. Men engaged in cleaning up. Full kit inspections made.	
	2		Battalion in tents as above. Weather dry & warm. A & B Companies are bathed at Divisional Baths in the village. C.O. holds a kit inspection of the men of the Battalion.	
	3		Battalion as above. Warning Order received to be prepared to move to the FORWARD AREA the following day to work on CORPS LINE.	
IN THE LINE	4		Battalion exclusive of Details moves to Forward Area. Tents are conveyed with the Battalion & pitched in valley EAST of HEDAUVILLE near the site of Work. Details carry on training of Lewis Gunners, Rifle Bombers, Scouts & Snipers, & Sanitary men.	
	5		Battalion in tents doing work on Corps line. Work from 2 A.M. till dawn.	
	6		do do	
	7		do do	

A5834 Wt. W4973/M687 750,000 8/16 D. D. & L. Ltd. Forms/C.2118/13

30. M.
5 shale

Army Form C. 2118.

Instructions regarding War Diaries and Intelligence Summaries are contained in F. S. Regs., Part II. and the Staff Manual respectively. Title pages will be prepared in manuscript.

WAR DIARY
or
INTELLIGENCE SUMMARY.
(Erase heading not required.)

Place	Date	Hour	Summary of Events and Information	Remarks and references to Appendices
	1918			
IN THE LINE	MAY 8		Battalion engaged in working on Corps Line. Details carry on with instruction of Specialists. Corps Commander presents Decorations to recipients as under:- MAJOR R.S. DIXON, D.S.O. — C.S.M. S. CARMICHAEL, D.C.M. MAJOR J. A. COX, D.S.O. — SERGT. G.M. HENRY, D.C.M. LIEUT. S. CAMPBELL, M.C. — SERGT. H. SMITH, M.M. 2/LT. A.I. WILLIAMSON, M.C. — CORPL. J. JAMIESON, M.M. 2/LT. J. CALLAN, M.C. — L/C. A. LAWLER, M.M.	
RUBEMPRÉ	9		Battalion returns to Tented Camp at RUBEMPRÉ. The following notifications appear in the London Gazette. CAPT. J. N. O. RYCROFT, D.S.O. M.C., ceased to hold the appointment of Brigade Major 106th I.B. (to command 12th H.L.I.) 17/4/18. T/MAJOR R. S. DIXON (CAPT. H.L.I.) to be acting Lt-Col. whilst commanding Battalion from 9th to 18th April 1918.	
	10		Battalion in RUBEMPRÉ. Intimation received that the award to A/Lt. Col. W. H. ANDERSON of the VICTORIA CROSS has been approved of by HIS MAJESTY THE KING.	

A5834 Wt. W4973/M687 750,000 8/16 D. D. & L. Ltd. Forms/C.2118/13

Instructions regarding War Diaries and Intelligence Summaries are contained in F. S. Regs., Part II. and the Staff Manual respectively. Title pages will be prepared in manuscript.

WAR DIARY
or
INTELLIGENCE SUMMARY.
(Erase heading not required.)

Army Form C. 2118.

Place	Date	Hour	Summary of Events and Information	Remarks and references to Appendices
	1918			
RUBEMPRÉ	MAY 11		Battalion in Tented Camp as above. Training carried on on various Areas allotted to the Battalion. Small ranges up to 200YDS. are made use of & practices carried on under the supervision of the Musketry Officer.	
	12		Battalion accommodated as above. Training carried on as above. Weather dry & very hot.	
	13		do do do	
	14		do do do	
	15		do do do	
	16		do do do	
	17		do do do Warning Order received to move to Forward Area.	
	18		Battalion moves into the Line in accordance with Orders received. Being in Brigade RESERVE on RIGHT SECTOR of the DIVISIONAL FRONT.	

A5834 Wt. W4973/M687 750,000 8/16 D. D. & L. Ltd. Forms/C.2118/13

Instructions regarding War Diaries and Intelligence Summaries are contained in F. S. Regs., Part II. and the Staff Manual respectively. Title pages will be prepared in manuscript.

WAR DIARY
or
INTELLIGENCE SUMMARY.
(Erase heading not required.)

Army Form C. 2118.

Place	Date 1918	Hour	Summary of Events and Information	Remarks and references to Appendices
IN THE LINE	MAY 19		Battalion in Brigade Reserve, & occupying dugouts on the HEDAUVILLE – SENLIS ROAD.	
	20		Battalion as above. The area in which the Battalion is stationed is subjected to severe gas-shelling, causing serious casualties to B Coy & H.Qrs Coy. M.O. & staff require to be evacuated to hospital.	
	21		Battalion moves from SENLIS area to Camp between HEDAUVILLE & FORCEVILLE. One Company (D Coy) is left forward as garrison of portion of CORPS LINE. BATTLE SURPLUS move to TALMAS where they are under the administration of the DIVISIONAL WING.	
	22		Ditto.	
	23		Ditto. Australian doctor joins to take place of Capt Campbell gassed.	
	24		Ditto. Very wet and cold.	
	25		Moved into AVELUY LEFT sector relieving 7th L.F. A B & C Coys in front line D Coy in reserve. Relief complete 12:30 am.	
	26		Normal. Enemy barrage started 4 pm [illegible] on our artillery & replying on S.O.S. lines at 5 pm approx.	
	27		Normal.	
	28		Btn H.Qrs shelled consistently with 5.9s & 7.7cm guns from 12 noon to 6.30 pm. A Coy successfully raid enemy post killing five of the enemy.	

A5834 Wt. W4973/M687 750,000 8/16 D. D. & L. Ltd. Forms/C.2118/13

Instructions regarding War Diaries and Intelligence Summaries are contained in F. S. Regs., Part II. and the Staff Manual respectively. Title pages will be prepared in manuscript.

WAR DIARY
or
INTELLIGENCE SUMMARY.

(Erase heading not required.)

Army Form C. 2118.

Place	Date	Hour	Summary of Events and Information	Remarks and references to Appendices
IN THE LINE	29		Very quiet morning day: but noisy towards dark & during relief. Relieved by 17th L.F. Relief complete 1:40 am. Proceed to camp between HEDAUVILLE & FORCEVILLE. A Coy left forward as garrison of portion of Purple system.	
	30		Cleaning up and resting in camp: weather hot.	
	31		Ditto ; ditto . Small amount of training done musketry, anti-gas & P.T.	
			Casualties between 21st & 31st inclusive:-	
			Killed: OR A Coy One; B Coy Nil; C Coy Nil; D Coy Nil; ~~HQrs~~ ~~Nil~~	
			Gassed OR A Coy 21; B " 60; C " 10; D " 16; ~~HQrs~~ " " [illegible]	
			Wounded OR A Coy 6; B " 3; C " 1; D " 7	
			Officers. Capt D J Watson gassed 21st.	
			Lieut W F Burton ditto 21st.	
			Capt T H Campbell ditto 21st. RAMC attached.	
			Lieut A Anderson ditto 21st.	
			Lieut A C Bethune ditto 21st.	
			Capt & Rev R H J Stewart ditto 21st.	
			Lieut S J Hearn gassed 25th	
			Lieut A McDougal wounded 27th	
			2 Lieut H Cowan gassed 27th	
			H Carter [illegible] Lieut A/Adjt 12 HLI.	

A5834 Wt. W4973/M687 750,000 8/16 D. D. & L. Ltd. Forms/C.2118/13

Instructions regarding War Diaries and Intelligence Summaries are contained in F. S. Regs., Part II. and the Staff Manual respectively. Title pages will be prepared in manuscript.

WAR DIARY
or
~~INTELLIGENCE SUMMARY.~~
(Erase heading not required.)

Army Form C. 2118.

12TH Bn. HIGH. L.I.

From 1st to 30th June 1918

Place	Date	Hour	Summary of Events and Information	Remarks and references to Appendices
FORCEVILLE	June 1st		Day spent in Bivouac camp preparing for [illegible]. Orders for relief changed at last moment and at dusk the Battn. moved up to relieve the 17th Lancashire Fusiliers in left sector AVELUY WOOD. Line taken over as vacated on 27th April. Companies are disposed as follows. 'C' Coy right front 'B' Coy centre 'A' Coy left front 'D' Coy Support. Headquarters on western edge of wood. Relief [illegible] carried out under [illegible] conditions. Two Coys taking few casualties. [illegible] weather.	
AVELUY WOOD.	2nd		Night passed quietly. Enemy [illegible] himself freely & snipers claimed [illegible] doubtful hits. [illegible] Coy passed quietly [illegible]. At [illegible] a.m. enemy bombarded our right Coy & the Battn on our right (15th High L.I.). [illegible] 8.45 a.m. A considerable number of gas shells were used. After "Stand Down" "D" Coy relieved "A" Coy in left front. "A" Coy moving into support. Relief completed without trouble. Night quiet with occasional bursts of [illegible] by enemy artillery & Machine Guns. A draft of 14 O.R. joined the Battn.	
	3rd		Companies active sniping [illegible] now more cautious in exposing themselves. Several hits claimed obtained. Invitation to [illegible] sent into our lines accompanied by a German newspaper giving an account of [illegible]. The vicinity of Bn. H.Q. shelled with 5.9 for an hour [illegible] morning. During the afternoon a heavy trench mortar fell in [illegible] between H.Q. and MARTINSART. Lt. W. T. McKellar was wounded. The Night passed quietly.	

A5834 Wt. W4973/M687 750,000 8/16 D. D. & L. Ltd. Forms/C.2118/13

31. M.

7 photos

Vol 31

35

Instructions regarding War Diaries and Intelligence Summaries are contained in F. S. Regs., Part II. and the Staff Manual respectively. Title pages will be prepared in manuscript.

WAR DIARY
or
INTELLIGENCE SUMMARY.
(Erase heading not required.)

Army Form C. 2118.

Place	Date	Hour	Summary of Events and Information	Remarks and references to Appendices
AVELUY WOOD.	June 4th	1918	At 2.30 A.M. enemy opened heavy Trench Mortar Bombardment on left Coy and on the Battn on our left. This lasted till 3.45 A.M. A few gas bombs were used only affecting a small area. Increased aerial activity at dawn [illegible] in the morning. Weather very warm & dry. Day quiet with artillery activity on back areas. Capt T. R. Willetts killed by M.G. fire and Lieut H. G. [illegible] wounded.	
	5th		Night passed quietly. Enemy field guns opening occasional bursts on tracks. Dry weather continues [illegible] quietly. Enemy strafe [illegible] of support Coy [illegible]. Captain T. G. Walton [illegible] rejoined from hospital. Night passed quietly [illegible] amount of M.G. activity. Lt G. F. Shiels [?] evacuated sick.	
	6th		Situation quiet. Weather continues dry & warm. Major J. M. O. Rycroft D.S.O. M.C. wounded, remaining at duty till relieved by Major R. S. DIXON D.S.O. M.C. [illegible] proceeded for rest to [illegible]. Captain G. T. CRAIK M.C. proceeded to [illegible] 46th Inf. Bde. "A" Coy relieved C Coy on the right after [illegible] and C Coy returned to Support. Night passed without incident.	
	7th		Morning quiet. Enemy Trench Mortars active on Support Coy area. Enemy shelled Battn. area very heavily between 11 p.m. & 11.15 p.m. Concentrating on various Company areas and [illegible] quarters.	

A5834 Wt. W4973/M687 750,000 8/16 D. D. & L. Ltd. Forms/C.2118/13

Instructions regarding War Diaries and Intelligence Summaries are contained in F. S. Regs., Part II. and the Staff Manual respectively. Title pages will be prepared in manuscript.

WAR DIARY
or
INTELLIGENCE SUMMARY.
(Erase heading not required.)

Army Form C. 2118.

Place	Date	Hour	Summary of Events and Information	Remarks and references to Appendices
AVELUY WOOD.	June 8th	1918.	Morning passed quietly till 9.30 A.M. When enemy started shelling [illegible] in ~~Support [illegible]~~ R.10 in vicinity of Battn. H.Q. & Support Coy. area with 5.9" continuing without interruption till 1 p.m. Shells used being fired at the rate of 6 per minute. Shelling resumed in the afternoon between 2 & 3.0 p.m. when retaliation by our heavies stopped it. Enemy remained quiet till we opened up a heavy bombardment on the South East side of AVELUY WOOD, clear of our front line trenches for it. Enemy retaliated [illegible] shelled heavily searching all the wood with his fire. [illegible] at 12.30 p.m. Draft of 148 O.Rs. reported for duty. 2nd Lts. [illegible] and E.T.R. Hannah were wounded.	
	9th		Stand to [illegible] with much [illegible]. Weather clear, dry & warm. Day very quiet. Slight change of weather towards evening. 2nd Lt. F.S. Sutherland was wounded.	
	10th		Heavy Artillery fire on Valley East of MARTINSART & in the [illegible] Battn. H.Q. at Stand-to [illegible] at 1.30 A.M. Day quiet [illegible] of rain in afternoon [illegible]. Evening [illegible] incident. Enemy shelled MARTINSART at Stand [illegible] area.	

A5834 Wt. W4973/M687 750,000 8/16 D. D. & L. Ltd. Forms/C.2118/13

Instructions regarding War Diaries and Intelligence Summaries are contained in F. S. Regs., Part II. and the Staff Manual respectively. Title pages will be prepared in manuscript.

WAR DIARY
or
INTELLIGENCE SUMMARY.
(Erase heading not required.)

Army Form C. 2118.

Place	Date	Hour	Summary of Events and Information	Remarks and references to Appendices
Aveluy Wood.	June 1918. 11th		Morning very quiet. At 2.30 p.m. very heavy [illegible] barrage put down on the Butts area [illegible]. The enemy under cover of the barrage raided one of our posts successfully for the first time. Two men were taken prisoner. Our posts in the neighbourhood opened rifle & Lewis Gun fire but the enemy got away with the prisoners. One [illegible] of the [illegible] wounded. The situation was normal by [illegible] p.m. [illegible] artillery [illegible] Stand-to [illegible] was cancelled in case of [illegible] having leaked out. Draft of [illegible] O.R.s arrive.	
	12th		Night passed uneventfully. Some shelling at Stand-to [illegible] day very quiet [illegible] M.G. fire at night. Major A.S. Dixon D.S.O. M.C. evacuated sick and Capt Houston takes over command.	
	13th		The day passed quietly. The [illegible] front 200x to the [illegible] and it is [illegible] in depth with two coys in front line finding their local supports, one coy in support and one in Reserve. [illegible] "A" Coy Right front. "C" Coy Left front. "D" Coy support. "B" Coy reserve. Headquarters west of MARTINSART. Lt. Col. [illegible] [illegible] over command of the Battn. Draft of 30 O.R.s report for duty.	

A5834 Wt. W4973/M687 750,000 8/16 D. D. & L. Ltd. Forms/C.2118/13

WAR DIARY
or
INTELLIGENCE SUMMARY.
(Erase heading not required.)

Army Form C. 2118.

Instructions regarding War Diaries and Intelligence Summaries are contained in F. S. Regs., Part II. and the Staff Manual respectively. Title pages will be prepared in manuscript.

Place	Date	Hour	Summary of Events and Information	Remarks and references to Appendices
AVELUY WOOD.	June 14th	1918	Day passed quietly. Bn H.Q. intermittently shelled. Warning order for relief received. Usual M.G. activity at night.	
	15th		Enemy very quiet except for increased aerial activity. Preparations made for handing over. 2nd Lieut. J. Cullen M.C. rejoined from hospital and Lieuts. H. W. Scott, R. B. Aitken and 2nd Lieut C. V. Newman report for duty.	
	16th		Day passed quietly. Relief by 7th Buffs. 12th Division commenced after dark.	
WARLOY.	17th		Relief slow and not complete till 2-30 a.m. The Battn proceeded to billets in [illegible]. The morning and afternoon were spent in cleaning up and at 4.30 p.m. the Battn marched to ARQUEVES where it arrived at 7 p.m. and went into billets. Total casualties during tour: 1 off. + 10 O.R.s killed, 6 off. + 74 O.R.s wounded, 2 O.R.s missing.	
ARQUEVES	18th		Reveille 7 a.m. Day spent cleaning up and kit inspections. Captain [illegible] assumes charge of Battn Supply [illegible] duties of 2/Lt [illegible].	
	19th		Reveille 6.30 a.m. Day spent in refitting. Parades under Coy arrangements. 2nd Lieut C. V. Newman evacuated sick. Weather showery.	
	20th		Morning Coy [illegible]. Drill, Lewis gun, P.T., Bayonet Fighting, Bombing etc. [illegible] carried out by Brigade Gas Officer and Brigade [illegible]. Weather fine and warm. 2nd Lieut J. W. Clements and [illegible] O.R.s reported for duty.	

47

Army Form C. 2118.

WAR DIARY
or
INTELLIGENCE SUMMARY.
(Erase heading not required.)

Instructions regarding War Diaries and Intelligence Summaries are contained in F. S. Regs., Part II. and the Staff Manual respectively. Title pages will be prepared in manuscript.

Place	Date	Hour	Summary of Events and Information	Remarks and references to Appendices
ARQUÈVES	June 21st	1918.	Training continued as above. Weather showery.	
	22nd		Training continued as much Range practice as possible being done.	
	23rd		Church Parade. The Major General presented ribbons of recently won decorations in front of the Brigade which formed three sides of a square. Major R.S. Dixon D.S.O., M.C. returned from hospital and Lieut W.D. McFarlane [illegible]. Lieut H.E. Bethune reported from Hospital. [illegible] reported for duty. [illegible]	
	24th		Training continued [illegible] Coy in attack also [illegible]. Draft of 23 O.Rs reported for duty.	
	25th		Training continued as above. Brigade transport inspected by the Major General, who gave them special praise and said it was best in the Division. [illegible]	
	26th		Training continued. A demonstration was given with Livens Gas Projectors. Lieut H.G. Nicholson returned from hospital.	
	27th		Training continued. Bullet & Bayonet competition held in Brigade. 1 team from each Coy entered. Team from D Coy was placed 2nd. Battn. placed on [illegible] hours notice from Midnight to 5 a.m. daily.	
	28th		Training continued. ~~Divisional rifle meeting~~ [illegible] afternoon. Meeting of all officers at Divisional H.Q. in evening. Lieut. K. Stewart evacuated to [illegible]. [illegible] with 50 yds of [illegible]	
	29th		[illegible] at short notice. Later orders to entrain at Doullens on 30th for unknown destination. Given later as ARQUES. Battn. Supplies moved to TALMAS at 5 p.m. under Major R.S. Dixon. Divisional Rifle Meeting held in afternoon at ARQUÈVES.	

Instructions regarding War Diaries and Intelligence Summaries are contained in F. S. Regs., Part II. and the Staff Manual respectively. Title pages will be prepared in manuscript.

WAR DIARY
or
INTELLIGENCE SUMMARY.
(Erase heading not required.)

Army Form C. 2118.

Place	Date	Hour	Summary of Events and Information	Remarks and references to Appendices
ARQUEVES	June 1918 30th.		Preparations made for move. "B" Coy proceeds Batt. leaving at 2-30 p.m. to do duty as unloading party at Detraining Station. Battn. marches off at 7 p.m. to entrain at Doullens Jnc. to leave DOULLENS at 11-20 p.m.	
			K. D. Dixon Major for Officer Cmdg. 1/9th Highland	

A5834 Wt. W4973/M687 750,000 8/16 D. D. & L. Ltd. Forms/C.2118/13

Instructions regarding War Diaries and Intelligence Summaries are contained in F. S. Regs., Part II. and the Staff Manual respectively. Title pages will be prepared in manuscript.

WAR DIARY
or
~~INTELLIGENCE SUMMARY.~~
(Erase heading not required.)

Army Form C. 2118.

~~19th H.L.I.~~

Vol 32

Place	Date	Hour	Summary of Events and Information	Remarks and references to Appendices
	1918			
ARQUIVES	JULY 1		Battalion proceeded to ARQUIES, arriving about 8 p.m. & thence marched to FORT ROUGE, where the men bivouaced for late breakfast. Men were subsequently marched to billets. Battle Surplus at WARNIES	
ZERMAZEELE	2		Order received to embus at RENESCURES about 6.30 A.M. & Battalion moved off at 7.10 pm. Thirty men are conveyed in one Motor Bus. At 6.50 pm. the Battalion arrive at ZERMAZEELE. Warning Order received to be prepared to move next day.	
	3		The Battalion move by march Route to WINNIZEELE arriving at 7.30 pm. & settling in billets in the village for the night. Warned to be ready to move the following morning.	[initials]
	4		The Battalion move by March Route to Q. 11 Central	

32. M. [illegible]

A5834 Wt. W4973/M687 750,000 8/16 D. D. & L. Ltd. Forms/C.2118/13

Army Form C. 2118.

Instructions regarding War Diaries and Intelligence Summaries are contained in F. S. Regs., Part II. and the Staff Manual respectively. Title pages will be prepared in manuscript.

WAR DIARY
or
INTELLIGENCE SUMMARY.
(Erase heading not required.)

Place	Date	Hour	Summary of Events and Information	Remarks and references to Appendices
	1918			
Near STEENVOORDE	JULY 4		(Sheet 27. Belgium & France) taking over from the French. Battalion in Brigade Reserve of Brigade in the Line & also at call of Corps. Relief complete by 11 pm. 35th Division now in XIX Corps, but subsequently transferred to X Corps.	
	5		Battalion in Billets near Q 11. Central. Weather dry & hot	
	6		do do	
	7		do do	
	8		do do Positions & areas of Companies in Support reconnoitred	[illegible]

A5834 Wt. W4973/M687 750,000 8/16 D. D. & L. Ltd. Forms/C.2118/13

Instructions regarding War Diaries and Intelligence Summaries are contained in F. S. Regs., Part II. and the Staff Manual respectively. Title pages will be prepared in manuscript.

WAR DIARY
or
INTELLIGENCE SUMMARY.
(Erase heading not required.)

Army Form C. 2118.

Place	Date	Hour	Summary of Events and Information	Remarks and references to Appendices
	1918			
IN RESERVE 5/27. B.11 Central	JULY 8		Orders received to relieve 17 Royal Scots in Support.	
	9		Battalion as above. Weather still dry, but thunder threatening. Advance Party proceed to Support Battalion Area to take over. Draft of 19 O.R. joined Battn. from Base. 2/LIEUT. T. F. MURRAY reported for duty & is posted to "B" Coy.	
	10		Battalion as above. During early morning a German aeroplane dropped several bombs in the vicinity of Battalion H.Qrs.	
	11		Battalion relieve 17th Royal Scots in Support. Relief complete by 12.45 pm. No casualties. Situation quiet.	[illegible initials]
	12		Companies distributed in Bivouacs in Support Area. "A" Company supply Working Party nightly to work in Forward Area, remaining Companies supplying parties	

A5834 Wt. W4973/M687 750,000 8/16 D. D. & L. Ltd. Forms/C.2118/13

Instructions regarding War Diaries and Intelligence Summaries are contained in F. S. Regs., Part II. and the Staff Manual respectively. Title pages will be prepared in manuscript.

WAR DIARY
or
INTELLIGENCE SUMMARY.
(*Erase heading not required.*)

Army Form C. 2118.

Place	Date	Hour	Summary of Events and Information	Remarks and references to Appendices
	1919		for work in Support Area & for carrying Wire, ammunition	
IN THE LINE	JULY 12		etc.	
	13		Battalion distributed as above. Situation quiet.	
	14		do do Desultory shelling on S.W. slope of Mt. VEDAIGNE from 10.30 AM. to 11.30.	
	15		Battalion as above. Warning Order received to relieve Royal Scots in Front System on night 16/17th July.	
	16		Battalion as above. Considerable hostile fire on back Areas. BAILLEUL being shelled by our guns in retaliation. At 4.45 five rounds of our own artillery hit a dump in the enemy lines causing explosions. Day otherwise quiet.	
	17		Relief of the Royal Scots in Front System LOCRE SUB-SECTOR of the 35th Divisional Front completed by 1.45 pm.	

A5834 Wt. W4973/M687 750,000 8/16 D. D. & L. Ltd. Forms/C.2118/13

Army Form C. 2118.

Instructions regarding War Diaries and Intelligence Summaries are contained in F. S. Regs., Part II. and the Staff Manual respectively. Title pages will be prepared in manuscript.

WAR DIARY
or
INTELLIGENCE SUMMARY.
(Erase heading not required.)

Place	Date	Hour	Summary of Events and Information	Remarks and references to Appendices
IN THE LINE	1918 JULY 17		Stand to quiet. At 9.48 A.M. the enemy opened Trench Mortar strafe on our Front Line. Draft of 20 O.R. received.	
	18		Battalion in the Line as above. During the course of the night 17/18th much artillery activity on the part of our guns in view of expected enemy attack. At 12.30 A.M. enemy put down a very accurate barrage on our Front Line. & again at 2.50 A.M. a very heavy Trench Mortar Barrage opened on our Front System & on the front of Division on our Right. S.O.S. reported at 2.59 A.M. on our RIGHT & sent through to Brigade. Bombardment continued until 3.40 A.M when the situation became quieter & at 4 A.M. front Line Companies reported situation normal.	
	19		Battalion in the Line as above. Weather broken & unsettled with heavy thunder showers.	[initials]

A5834 Wt. W4973/M687 750,000 8/16 D. D. & L. Ltd. Forms/C.2118/13

Instructions regarding War Diaries and Intelligence Summaries are contained in F. S. Regs., Part II. and the Staff Manual respectively. Title pages will be prepared in manuscript.

WAR DIARY
or
INTELLIGENCE SUMMARY.
(Erase heading not required.)

Army Form C. 2118.

Place	Date	Hour	Summary of Events and Information	Remarks and references to Appendices
IN THE LINE	1918 JULY 19		Aviation throughout the day quiet. Enemy aerial activity about 8 A.M. over our lines. Throughout the night our artillery kept up harassing fire on enemy lines. Several patrols who went out to locate enemy posts, found several posts unoccupied.	
	20		Battalion in the line as above. Arrangements made for the occupation of enemy posts & operation carried out successfully. Booby traps consisting of quantities of explosive found in several of the posts & destroyed. No attempt on the part of the enemy to recapture posts. LIEUT. H. M. SCOTT evacuated, wounded. Draft of 11 O.R. received	
	21		Battalion in the line as above. Weather during morning very wet & front line consequently very unpleasant, some of the Posts having 6 to 8 inches of water. Dry socks sent up so that when the Posts get dry the men	[illegible]

Instructions regarding War Diaries and Intelligence Summaries are contained in F. S. Regs., Part II. and the Staff Manual respectively. Title pages will be prepared in manuscript.

WAR DIARY
or
INTELLIGENCE SUMMARY.
(Erase heading not required.)

Army Form C. 2118.

Place	Date 1918	Hour	Summary of Events and Information	Remarks and references to Appendices
IN THE LINE	JULY 21		may have a dry change. Orders issued for the relief of the Battalion by the 18th H.L.I.	
	22		Battalion in billets in Reserve. Relief completed by 1 A.M. & all Companies settled in by 3 A.M.	
	23		Battalion in Reserve. Men occupied in cleaning up & resting. Situation quiet. Enemy artillery quiet. Draft of 10 O.R. received from Divisional Reception Camp.	
	24		Battalion in Reserve. Weather unsettled with thunder. Reconnaissances of Front Line for proposed future Operations carried out by two Officers & four N.C.O.s per Company. Total Casualties for tour 22 O.R. wounded 1 O.R. killed.	[signature]
	25		The Battalion is relieved by the 2/16th County of London Regiment & move by March Route to EECKE area arriving about 7 pm. Officers & men accommodated in Farms. Draft of 61 O.R. received from Base	

A5834 Wt. W4973/M687 750,000 8/16 D. D. & L. Ltd. Forms/C.2118/13

Army Form C. 2118.

Instructions regarding War Diaries and Intelligence Summaries are contained in F. S. Regs., Part II. and the Staff Manual respectively. Title pages will be prepared in manuscript.

WAR DIARY
or
INTELLIGENCE SUMMARY.
(Erase heading not required.)

Place	Date	Hour	Summary of Events and Information	Remarks and references to Appendices
	1918			
IN THE LINE	JULY 26		Battalion accomodated as above. Men resting and cleaning	
	27		do. Men start training for small Operation to be carried out by 106th I.B.	
	28		Battalion accomodated as above. Men engaged in training. Ground staked off & men told off to various area. Weather unsettled with heavy showers.	
	29		Battalion accomodated as above, & engaged in training over taped area. Draft of 40 O.R. received from Divl Reception Camp	
	30		Battalion as above. Weather dry & warm. Night Operations carried out on Training Area	[illegible]
	31		Battalion as above. Day dry & very warm. Short Parade Service held for the Battalion.	

[illegible signature]

Instructions regarding War Diaries and Intelligence Summaries are contained in F. S. Regs., Part II. and the Staff Manual respectively. Title pages will be prepared in manuscript.

WAR DIARY
or
~~INTELLIGENCE SUMMARY.~~
(Erase heading not required.)

12th Bn. H. L. I.

August 1918

Army Form C. 2118.

35

9/R 33

Place	Date	Hour	Summary of Events and Information	Remarks and references to Appendices
	1918			
IN THE LINE	AUG^T 1		Battalion in Support Area awaiting notification of ZERO hour & day. Weather very wet all day, rendering ground quite impassible. Operations Order for proposed minor operation attached and marked K	
	2		ZERO day. Ground so wet that Division decide that proposed operation be postponed till a more favourable opportunity shows itself. Day unsettled with more rain.	
	3		Battalion moves from Support Area to RESERVE & are accomodated in bivouacs. LIEUTS. LAMB & WILLIAMSON proceed to England for Tour of Duty.	
	4		Battalion as above. Situation quiet. No casualties during tour of one day & two nights. Three other ranks wounded on moving into Reserve Area.	
	5		Battalion as above warned to move at 9.30 pm & occupy positions of assembly. Move into position takes place without incident or mishap.	

33. M.
5 sheets

A7092. Wt W128 9/M1293 750,000. 1/17. D. D & L., Ltd. Forms/C2118/14.

Instructions regarding War Diaries and Intelligence Summaries are contained in F. S. Regs., Part II. and the Staff Manual respectively. Title pages will be prepared in manuscript.

WAR DIARY

or

~~INTELLIGENCE SUMMARY.~~

(Erase heading not required.)

Army Form C. 2118.

Place	Date	Hour	Summary of Events and Information	Remarks and references to Appendices
	1918			
IN THE LINE	AUG. 6		Battalion in Support Area awaiting Orders to attack. Day was wet.	
	7		Battalion as above. Orders received to cancel proposed Operation. LIEUT. H.H. Scott rejoins the Battalion from Hospital.	
	8		Battalion moves into line taking over from 1/6th Cheshires in the CENTRE Section, LOCRE SUB-SECTOR. Relief complete by 2.15 A.M.	
	9		Battalion in the line as above. Situation quiet with occasional Shelling of Front Area.	
	10		Battalion holding the line as above. Orders for relief of the Battalion in the line by 2/15th London received.	
	11		Battalion moves into RESERVE AREA & are accomodated in BIVOUACS, moving the same evening into area South of STEENVOORDE, H.Qrs at Q.2.c. central & Companies scattered in farms in the vicinity.	
	12		Battalion as above. Men engaged in cleaning & resting. Weather dry & warm. Draft of 5 O.R. received.	

A7092. Wt. W128 g/M1293 750,000. 1/17. D. D. & L., Ltd. Forms/C2118/14.

Army Form C. 2118.

Instructions regarding War Diaries and Intelligence Summaries are contained in F. S. Regs., Part II. and the Staff Manual respectively. Title pages will be prepared in manuscript.

WAR DIARY
or
~~INTELLIGENCE SUMMARY~~.
(Erase heading not required.)

Place	Date	Hour	Summary of Events and Information	Remarks and references to Appendices
~~1918~~ STEENVOORDE	1919 AUG. 13		Battalion as above. Companies engaged in reorganising & refitting. Draft of 90 O.R. received. 2/LIEUT. O.V. HARLAND joins Battalion & is attached to T.M. Battery.	
	14		Battalion as above. Companies engaged in training. Small range available on which Companies in rotation engage in Firing Practices at 30 yds. 2/LIEUT. W.C. COOPER joins Battalion & is posted to "A" Coy.	
	15		Battalion in billets & bivouacs as above. Weather dry & very hot.	
	16		Ditto Ditto Working Party supplied by "D" Coy. – two Officers & 90 men – for Forward Area. Ditto	
	17		Ditto Ditto	
	18		Ditto Ditto	
	19		Ditto	
	20		Ditto Ditto	

A7092. Wt. W128 9/M1293 750,000. 1/17. D. D. & L., Ltd. Forms/C2118/14.

Instructions regarding War Diaries and Intelligence Summaries are contained in F. S. Regs., Part II. and the Staff Manual respectively. Title pages will be prepared in manuscript.

WAR DIARY

or

~~INTELLIGENCE SUMMARY.~~

(*Erase heading not required.*)

Army Form C. 2118.

Place	Date	Hour	Summary of Events and Information	Remarks and references to Appendices
	1918			
STEENVOORDE	AUG 21		Battalion in billets & in bivouacs. Companies engaged in training by Sections & Platoons. One Company per day on the range, firing elementary practices at 30 YDS.	
	22		Ditto Ditto	
	23		Ditto Ditto	
	24		Ditto Ditto	
	~~25~~		During the afternoon & evening the Battalion holds a Sports Day. Some of the principal events with Winners are given below,–	
			1 Mile Race Corpl. Brown A Coy.	
			100 YDS Race Corpl. Hunter B Coy.	
			Tug of War H.Qrs. Coy.	
			5 a side Football A Coy. 11 a side Football "C" Coy.	
			Officers Scurry Race on Mules 1st Major R. S. DIXON, D.S.O.	
			Officers 100 YDS Race Capt. Carpenter.	

A7092 Wt. W128 9/M1293 750,000 1/17. D. D & L., Ltd. Forms/C2118/14.

Instructions regarding War Diaries and Intelligence Summaries are contained in F. S. Regs., Part II. and the Staff Manual respectively. Title pages will be prepared in manuscript.

Army Form C. 2118.

WAR DIARY

or

~~INTELLIGENCE SUMMARY.~~

(Erase heading not required.)

Place	Date 1919	Hour	Summary of Events and Information	Remarks and references to Appendices
STEENVOORDE	AUG. 25		Battalion in billets as above. Joint Church Parade of Presbyterians & C. of Eng. in field in vicinity of 'B' Coys. billet.	
	26		Battalion as above engaged in Musketry & General Training	
	27		do LIEUT. H.P. McDOUGALD joins Battalion & is posted to 'D' Company	
	28		Battalion as above, engaged in Musketry & General Training. do	
	29		do	
	30		Battalion warned to move into line, taking over from 1st Royal INNISKILLIN FUSILIERS. All arrangements completed when relief cancelled, & advance parties recalled.	
	31		Battalion in Billets as above. Training carried on as above.	[illegible]

[illegible] Capt

A7092. Wt W128 9/M1293 750,000. 1/17. D. D & L., Ltd. Forms/C2118/14.

Instructions regarding War Diaries and Intelligence Summaries are contained in F. S. Regs., Part II. and the Staff Manual respectively. Title pages will be prepared in manuscript.

106/36

Army Form C. 2118.

35

WAR DIARY

~~or~~

~~INTELLIGENCE~~ SUMMARY.

(Erase heading not required.)

12 HLI

Vol 34

Place	Date	Hour	Summary of Events and Information	Remarks and references to Appendices
STEENVORDE	1/9/18	—	Orders to take over CROIX-DE-POPERINGHE sector being cancelled the Btn remained at rest outside STEENVORDE: at 8:30 am orders are recieved for reconnoitring parties to proceed by lorry to the ~~[illegible]~~ CANAL sector which the Btn was to take over on night 3rd/4th. Further orders are recieved ordering the Bde to move the following day to ROAD CAMP.	
EN ROUTE to	2/9/18	—	Btn moves off at 9:30 am following Bde H.Qrs: weather during march is good & billets on arrival at ROAD CAMP are good being Nissen Huts. Battle Surplus still at ARNEKE.	
ROAD CAMP	3/9/18	—	Btn is to take over the CANAL Sector from the 119th (American) Regiment during night 3rd/4th. All preparations are made & Btn moves in two halves one at 4:30 pm & one at ~~4~~ 4:40 pm trains left BLUEGRASS at 6:30 & 6:40 pm respectively. Transport lines ~~and~~ and Q.M. stores remained at ROAD CAMP. Relief proceeds A & D front line B reserve & support.	
LINE	4/9/18	—	At 3:40 am relief is complete, having been a quiet one but later the enemy shells our reserve trenches with gas which results in about 20 casualties. Daylight patrols are ordered ~~from~~ the two front line companies namely A and D Coys. These patrols get out about 1000 yds towards the enemy before they are forced to withdraw having had a Lewis Gun knocked out & one man wounded. During this tour in the line daylight patrols of some considerable strength are frequent & produce	34.M. [illegible]

2353 Wt. W2544/1454 700,000 5/15 D. D. & L. A.D.S.S./Forms/C. 2118.

Instructions regarding War Diaries and Intelligence Summaries are contained in F. S. Regs., Part II. and the Staff Manual respectively. Title pages will be prepared in manuscript.

WAR DIARY
or
~~INTELLIGENCE SUMMARY.~~

(Erase heading not required.)

Army Form C. 2118.

Place	Date	Hour	Summary of Events and Information	Remarks and references to Appendices
LINE	4/9/18	Cont	some ~~[illegible]~~ good results which included a letter of congratulation from the Brigadier General on the work done by ~~the~~ Lieut J. S. YOUNG, and Lieut HE BETHUNE who were in command of the two patrols mentioned in the preceding paragraph.	
LINE	5/9/18	—	4:30am ~~[illegible]~~ QM & Hon Capt J. Carpenter proceeds on leave from transport lines which remain at ROAD CAMP until the 8th. 5:30am till 7:30am enemy TM's active on right front Coy area and again from 8-9pm. A heavy bombardment with "whizzbangs" and 4.2's on the left Coy area commences at 5:30am & continues till 6:30am: this is repeated at 3:30pm till 5pm, during which Lieut HE BETHUNE is wounded but remains at duty. Night patrols are sent out. A Coy water party is shelled at water point during night & two men are killed & 8 wounded.	
	6/9/18		Heavy shelling of right Company Head Quarters between 1.30 & 3 p.m. Day-light patrols were ordered and went out at 5 p.m. from Front Line Companies under Lieuts. BETHUNE & SCOTT. Left Company patrol got out as far as SPOIL BANK which was found to be unoccupied and the right Company patrol got out 500 yards. At this point the enemy	[initials]

Instructions regarding War Diaries and Intelligence Summaries are contained in F. S. Regs., Part II. and the Staff Manual respectively. Title pages will be prepared in manuscript.

WAR DIARY
or
INTELLIGENCE SUMMARY.
(Erase heading not required.)

Army Form C. 2118.

Place	Date	Hour	Summary of Events and Information	Remarks and references to Appendices
	1918			
IN THE LINE	SEP. 6		put down a barrage on both patrols, right Company having two men killed and one wounded, left Company one officer Lieut. Scott, killed, & one man missing. The Battalion is relieved by the 17th Royal Scots on the night of 6/7th, & Battalion are reported in billets by 1.30 AM.	
POPERINGHE	7		Battalion in Billets S.E. of POPERINGHE. Weather dry & cold	
	8		Battalion as above. Resting & cleaning up.	
	9		do do	
	10		do do	
	11		do do	
	12		Battalion move forward to Brigade Support & are accomodated in KRUISSTRAAT AREA. Companies engaged in reorganising, & refitting.	
	13		do do	
	14		do do	
	15		do do	[signature]

2353 Wt. W2544/1454 700,000 5/15 D. D. & L. A.D.S.S./Forms/C. 2118.

Instructions regarding War Diaries and Intelligence Summaries are contained in F. S. Regs., Part II. and the Staff Manual respectively. Title pages will be prepared in manuscript.

WAR DIARY
or
INTELLIGENCE SUMMARY.

(Erase heading not required.)

Army Form C. 2118.

Place	Date	Hour	Summary of Events and Information	Remarks and references to Appendices
	1918			
KRUISSTRAAT	SEPT. 16 17		Battalion in Brigade Support as above. Intermittent shelling all day & night by H.V. Guns from direction of GHELUVELT. Various working & carrying parties furnished by the Battalion. Weather dry & cold	
	18		ditto	
	19		ditto	
	20		ditto	
	21		ditto	
	22		ditto	
	23		ditto	
	24		ditto	
	25		ditto	
	26		ditto	
	27 28		Battalion move up to Sector South of ZILLEBEKE LAKE in preparation for attack to be carried out on the following day under orders of 106th I.B.	[illegible]

2353 Wt. W2544/1454 700,000 5/15 D. D. & L. A.D.S.S./Forms/C. 2118.

Instructions regarding War Diaries and Intelligence Summaries are contained in F. S. Regs., Part II. and the Staff Manual respectively. Title pages will be prepared in manuscript.

WAR DIARY
or
INTELLIGENCE SUMMARY.
(Erase heading not required.)

Army Form C. 2118.

Place	Date	Hour	Summary of Events and Information	Remarks and references to Appendices
IN THE LINE	1918 SEP. 28		Attack carried out in accordance with Brigade Orders. ZERO HOUR 5.30 A.M. All objectives gained.	
	29		Attack continued under Brigade Orders	
	30		do do	

D. Campbell Lieut
A/Adj. for C.O.

A7092. Wt W128 9/M1293 750,000. 1/17. D. D. & L., Ltd. Forms/C2118/14.

SECRET.

12th Battalion Highland Light Infantry.

OPERATION ORDER No. 34.

3rd Sept. 1918.

- -

1. The 106th Infantry Brigade will relieve the 119th American Regiment on the night of 3rd/4th in CANAL SECTOR of the Corps Front.

2. The 12th H.L.I. will relieve three companies of the 1st Battn. 119th Regt. forward of Battn. Hqrs. on LEFT FRONT.

3. Companies will be disposed as follows:-
   Right front - "A" Coy.) Relieving one America Coy. in
   Left Front - "D" ") Front Line.
   Support Coy.- "C" " Relieving one America Coy. in Support in old Front Line.
   Reserve Coy.- "D" " Relieving one American Coy. in area H.30.b. and I.25.a.

4. Front Line Companies will have three platoons in line and one in immediate support.

5. BOUNDARIES.
   Battalion Boundaries are as follows:-
   Right - I.31.d.30.35
   Left - I.32.a.65.55
   Inter Company Boundary - I.31.d.9.9.

6. GUIDES.
   One guide per platoon will meet platoons at 8 p.m. at Road Junction H.22.a.3.9.

7. All Air Photos, defence schemes, schemes of work, S.O.S. Signals, S.A.A. and Trench Stores will be taken over and receipts given. Receipts will be forwarded to Battn. Hqrs. by 9 a.m. 4th Sept.

8. Men's Packs, Officers' Valises and surplus Mess Gear will be handed in to Quartermasters Stores under supervision of Quartermaster, men's packs by 2.30 p.m., valises and mess gear by 3.30 p.m.

9. One Limber will report at Quartermaster's Stores at 3 p.m. to-day to convey Mess Gear for the Line, heavy Signalling Gear and M.O. Stores. This limber will be ready to move at 4 p.m.

10. Lewis Guns will be drawn and carried by the men.

11. ENTRAINMENT.
    Entraining will be carried out in accordance with attached table.

12. MARCH DISCIPLINE.
    The following distances on the march to entraining station will be maintained.:-
    500 yards between Battalions.
    100 " " Companies.
    50 " " Platoons.

13. Transport and Quartermaster's Stores will remain at present location until further orders.

14./

14. Completion of Relief will be reported to Battalion Hqrs. by code figures "214".

- -

ENTRAINING TABLE.

1st Train:-

Companies.	"A", "D" and 2 platoons and Coy. Hqrs. of "C" Coy.
Carrying	360 o.r. 12th H.L.I. 60 o.r. Brigade Hqrs.
Train Starts.	6.30 p.m.
From	BLUEGRASS (O.F.28.a.2.0.)
To	Yale (H.15.d.0.4.)

Lieut. Young is detailed as Entraining Officer for No. 1 Train.

2nd Train:-

Companies.	"B" and Hqrs. Coy. and 2 remaining platoons of "C" Coy.
Carrying	225 o.r. 12th H.L.I. 185 o.r. 18th H.L.I.
Train Starts	6.40 p.m.
From	BLUEGRASS.
To	YALE.

Lieut. Bryson is detailed as Entraining Officer for No. 2 train.

The Battalion will parade by Companies at 4.30 p.m. moving off in time to reach BLUEGRASS STATION half an hour before their train is due to leave in the following order:-

"A", "D" and 2 platoons "C" Coy.

and ten minutes later :-

Hqrs Coy. 2 platoons "C" Coy. and "B" Coy.

~~(Sd.) H. Carter Jones,~~

(Sd. S. Campbell, Lieut. & A/Adjt.
12th H.L.I.

Copies :-

All Companies.
Quartermaster.
Transport Sergt.
File.

SECRET. 12th Battalion Highland Light Infantry.

OPERATION ORDERS No. 36. 8/9/18.

---

1. An Inter-Battalion relief will be carried out to-morrow night in Right Sector of the Divisional Front.

2. 12th H.L.I. will relieve the 18th H.L.I. with Hqrs. at H.30.a.7.9.

3. DISPOSITIONS.
"B" Company will relieve "Z" Company on Right.
"C" " " "W" " Left.
"D" " " "Y" " Support.
"A" " " "X" " Reserve.

4. GUIDES to meet the Battalion will rendez vous at CAFE BELGE, H.29.b.8.5. at 8.30 p.m. - one man per platoon and one for Battn. Hqrs.

5. Companies will pick up guides in the following order, moving off as under:-
"B" Coy. - 8.15 p.m. "C" Coy. - 7.45 p.m.
"D" " - 8 p.m. "A" " - 8.15 p.m.
Hqrs. - 8.30 p.m.

6. ROUTE.
For "C", "D", "A" & Hqrs Coy. - VLAMERTINGHE - KRUISSTAATHOEK road.
For "B" Coy - Route at discretion of Company Commander.

7. RATIONS, for to-morrow will be brought to PIONEER JUNCTION by limber not later than 7 p.m. Companies' Ration Parties will be in waiting and rations will be distributed to the men before moving off. Rations for subsequent days will be sent up to WHITE HOUSE Station and distributed as before by Reserve Coy.

8. WATER.
15 full tins per Company will be taken by Companies into the Line to-morrow night. Water will be obtained subsequently at Water Tanks at WHITE HOUSE behind R.A.P. Companies will provide their own Water Parties.

9. COOKING.
No cooking will be carried out by Companies forward of Support Company. Reserve Company will carry in with them Company dixies and will be accompanied by Company Cooks. Dixies from all other Companies and Company Cooks will meet limbers bringing rations and return to Transport Lines with them.

10. All Air Photos, Defence Schemes, Schemes of Work, Trench Stores, etc. will be taken over and receipts given.
Trench Stores, etc. in present area will be carefully handed over and receipts obtained.
Receipts and lists will be handed in to Battn. Hqrs. by 2 p.m. 10th inst:

11. Advance Party for the Line already detailed.
Advance party to take over present Camp will report to Companies to-morrow afternoon.

12. /

12. **MARCH DISCIPLINE.**
The usual distances will be maintained between Companies and platoons on the march.

13. Company Billets and Areas will be left in a clean and sanitary condition.

14. Completion of relief will be reported to Battn. H.qrs., the code word TOP-DOG being used.

(Sd.) S. Campbell, Lieut. & A/Adjt.
12th H.L.I.

12th H.L.I.

Operation Order[s]

4 Sept. 1918

Ref Sheet 28 N.W.
" " S.W.

1. Information. In the event of 41st Division moving forward towards the MESSINES – ST ELOI Road, the 106th I.B. will advance and hold the ST ELOI – LOCK 8 Road.

2. Intention. The 12th H.L.I. will capture and hold a line from Cross Roads I.32.d.0.3 (inclusive) to Lock 8 (inclusive)

3 Boundaries. The boundary between 12th H.L.I. and 18th H.L.I. will be I.31.d.25.40. – I.32.d.0.3.
The boundary between Coys. will be I.31.b.95.05. – I.32.d.1.7.

4. Instructions
(a) A Coy will attack on the right and (B) Coy on the left.
(b) Coys. will attack on a two platoon front, holding 2 platoons in

4. Instructions.

(a) A Coy. will send out 1 patrol, and D Coy. 2 patrols.

(b) A Coys patrol will reconnoitre old french trench between BUS HOUSE inclusive and cross roads I.37.d.a.3. inclusive, then CONVENT LANE, WHITE HORSE CELLARS, SHELL LANE and SHELLEY FARM.

D Coys right patrol will reconnoitre old french trench East of the ST ELOI LOCK 8 road towards ARUNDAL and ground to North of it.

D Coys left patrol will reconnoitre the Canal Bank to Lock 7 then to Spoil Bank.

(c) Patrols will be prepared to give each other mutual assistance in dealing with enemy posts, and Coys. will be prepared to back up their patrols.

(d) Coys will hold platoons in readiness to follow up and make good ground won by patrols, A Coy. first making good old french trench, and D Coy. the ST ELOI - LOCK 8 Road.
The Second General Line to be made good

4

(4) Strength of Patrols should consist of between 10 and 15 ORs under an officer. D Coy will employ one good Sergeant to command one of the patrols.

5 Patrols will leave trenches at 5 pm.

6 Acknowledge.

(sd) S. Campbell Lt adjt
12 HLI

grid will be ST ELOI – LUCKY, and the third SHELLEY FARM – SPOIL BANK. As much use as possible will be made of existing trenches.

(e) Artillery will not fire East of the following line. SHELLEY FARM thence along GRIDLINE between O.2 and O.3 and I.32 and I.33 to MIDDLESEX Rd., then along MIDDLESEX Road.

(f) Dress Battle Order. Platoons will carry forward picks, shovels and flares.

(g) C Coy will be prepared to occupy positions vacated by A & D Coys and B Coy positions vacated by C Coy on receiving orders from HQrs.

(h) Patrols will keep Coy Commanders fully informed of their position, and Coys will keep HQrs fully informed of the situation.

(i) <u>Liaison</u>
Close liaison will be maintained between Coys. A Coy will maintain close touch with 18th H.L.I. on right and D Coy will keep the Coy on their left fully informed of their position.

(j)

Instructions regarding War Diaries and Intelligence Summaries are contained in F. S. Regs., Part II. and the Staff Manual respectively. Title pages will be prepared in manuscript.

WAR DIARY
or
INTELLIGENCE SUMMARY.
(Erase heading not required.)

12th Bn. H.L.I.

October 1918

Army Form C. 2118.

Vol 35

Place	Date	Hour	Summary of Events and Information	Remarks and references to Appendices
IN THE LINE	1918 Octr 1		Offensive Operations commenced on 28th ult. of which narrative is attached, continue. Weather very wet & stormy. Transport Lines & Qm. Stores move forward to RAILWAY EMBANKMENT, ONE KILOMETRE S. of YPRES.	
			The following officers join the Battalion for duty, 2/LIEUTS D.S. GRAY and A.M. OLIPHANT on the 26/9/18, & 2/LIEUT. J. GRAY on 30/9/18	
	2		Battalion are relieved on night 1/2nd Oct. by 7th R.I.R. & move to area two KILOMETRES E. of GHELUVELT where the day is spent.	
	3		At 7 AM. the Battalion move by march Route to KRUISSTRAAT area, three kilometres S.W. of YPRES & are accomodated in NISSEM HUTS and in bivouacs.	
			Total casualties during offensive Operations 28 Sep/1st Oct. amount to 5 Officers & 188 O.R. made up as follows.-	
			MAJOR J. A. COX, D.S.O. KILLED 29/9/18	
			CAPTAIN P. B. MILLIGAN KILLED 30/9/18	
			LIEUT. H. E. BETHUNE, M.C. KILLED 30/9/18	
			2/LIEUT. T. F. MURRAY WOUNDED 30/9/18	
			CAPT. R. F. MATHER WOUNDED 1/10/18	
			Other ranks 20 killed, 176 wounded & 12 missing.	

A5834 Wt. W4973/M687 750,000 8/16 D. D. & L. Ltd. Forms/C.2118/13

35 M
18 sheets

Instructions regarding War Diaries and Intelligence Summaries are contained in F. S. Regs., Part II. and the Staff Manual respectively. Title pages will be prepared in manuscript.

WAR DIARY
or
INTELLIGENCE SUMMARY.
(Erase heading not required.)

Army Form C. 2118.

Place	Date 1918	Hour	Summary of Events and Information	Remarks and references to Appendices
KRUISSTRAAT AREA	OCT. 4		Battalion in billets & bivouacs resting.	
			Major R.S. DIXON, D.S.O. M.C. proceeded to England to attend Commanding Officers Course at ALDERSHOT, assembling 6 Oct. 1918.	
			MAJOR D.G. WATSON, M.C., attached to 106th Infantry Brigade is appointed 2nd in command of 5th Camerons.	
			T/CAPT. H. CARTER JONAS is appointed ADJUTANT of the Battalion with effect from 27/3/18.	
			The following Honours and Awards are notified as having been given by the Corps Commander to Officers & Men of the Battalion.	
			MILITARY CROSS — T/LIEUT. H.E. BETHUNE (since killed in action)	
			BAR to MILITARY MEDAL — No. 22264, Sergt. D.G. O'HEA, M.M. (since died of wounds)	
			MILITARY MEDAL — No 34922 L/C. C. NICHOLAS	
			332997 D. RULE	
			23973 Cpl. W. BROWN	
	5		Battalion in billets & bivouacs as above. Companies engaged in re-equipping & reorganising.	
			Weather dry but threatening.	

A5834 Wt. W4973/M687 750,000 8/16 D. D. & L. Ltd. Forms/C.2118/13

Instructions regarding War Diaries and Intelligence Summaries are contained in F. S. Regs., Part II. and the Staff Manual respectively. Title pages will be prepared in manuscript.

WAR DIARY
or
~~INTELLIGENCE SUMMARY~~.
(Erase heading not required.)

Army Form C. 2118.

Place	Date 1918	Hour	Summary of Events and Information	Remarks and references to Appendices
KRUISSTRAAT	OCT 6		Battalion in billets & bivouacs. Brigade Joint Church Parade held which is attended by B.G.C. & staff.	
	7		Battalion in billets and bivouacs as above. Companies engaged in reorganising & re-equipping	
	8		ditto ditto. Weather wet & threatening	
	9		ditto Weather wet & showery. Capt J. TROTTER joins the Battalion & is given command of "D" Company.	
IN THE LINE	10		Battalion moves forward to K.20.a. in support to 100th & 105th Infantry Brigades, who are attacking.	
	~~11~~		2/LIEUTS. J.E. ALLEN, G.W. ROSS, & W. ADAM join Battalion for duty	
	11		Battalion as above accomodated in farms & Villages Shelling intermittent & principally from H.V. guns	
	12		Battalion as above. 2/Lt J.S. DOCHERTY joins the Battalion & posted for duty to "B" Company	
	13		Battalion as above. Warning Order received to prepare to move forward in support of 104 & 106 Infantry Brigades	

A5834 Wt. W4973/M687 750,000 8/16 D. D. & L. Ltd. Forms/C.2118/13.

Instructions regarding War Diaries and Intelligence Summaries are contained in F. S. Regs., Part II. and the Staff Manual respectively. Title pages will be prepared in manuscript.

WAR DIARY
or
INTELLIGENCE SUMMARY.
(Erase heading not required.)

Army Form C. 2118.

Place	Date	Hour	Summary of Events and Information	Remarks and references to Appendices
THE LINE	1918 Oct. 14		As per attached narrative, transport & Qr. Stores move forward to Our Front Line. Details in YPRES RAMPARTS.	
	14/21		As per attached narrative. During this period no drafts of reinforcements were received except casuals – men returning from leave & courses.	
			Capt. Crichton, O.C. B Company was evacuated to Hospital on 14/10/18. LIEUT. R B AITKEN on the 10/10/18 & 2/LIEUT. J E ALLAN on the 13/10/18. LIEUT. H.S.D. SMITH, O.C. C Company evacuated with G.S.W. on the 15th inst.	
			On the 21st intimation received of the following Awards for Services in the Field	
			<u>Military Medal</u> to 14962 L/C J. DOUGLAS, 8899, Pte. J. BLACK, 30825, L/Sgt. J. PHILLIPS, 40075, L/C R. HARVEY, 3991, PTE T. MOSS, 24715, " J. WALLACE, 8965, Pte T. BETTLEY, 18727, " A. GOODFELLOW, 16500, " W. WHITTLE, 8776 " D. McLELLAND, 41036, " W. BRADY, 31605, " D. WRIGHT	

A5834 Wt. W4973/M687 750,000 8/16 D. D. & L. Ltd. Forms/C.2118/13

Instructions regarding War Diaries and Intelligence Summaries are contained in F. S. Regs., Part II. and the Staff Manual respectively. Title pages will be prepared in manuscript.

WAR DIARY
or
INTELLIGENCE SUMMARY.

(Erase heading not required.)

Army Form C. 2118.

Place	Date	Hour	Summary of Events and Information	Remarks and references to Appendices
IN THE LINE	1919 OCT 22		Battalion moves into area S.E. of COURTRAI & are billeted in Area N.4 in farms & outskirts of COURTRAI. 38th Division now in CORPS RESERVE 2/LIEUT. J. E. LAING joins Battalion & is given command of "C" Coy during absence of LIEUT. H. S. D. SMITH.	
	23		Battalion as above, engaged in cleaning & resting. Weather dry.	
	24		Battalion as above. ditto ditto	
	25		Draft of 18 arrived. Warning Order received about midday to be ready to move at short notice. Move takes place at 4pm & Brigade move to SWEVEGHEM being in reserve to 41st Division. All Companies accomodated in billets in village by 7pm. The following Honours & Award notified in Orders. - The Military Cross T/2/LIEUT. H. W. STRUTHERS, LIEUT. R. B. AITKEN, LIEUT. J. C. ROBERTSON BAR to MILITARY CROSS LIEUT. J. CALLAN, M.C. Distinguished Conduct Medal No. 23097, Pte (L/c) J. WALKER 24429, C.S.M. R. CRAWFORD	

A7092 Wt W128 9/M1293 750,000. 1/17. D. D & L., Ltd. Forms/C2118/14.

Instructions regarding War Diaries and Intelligence Summaries are contained in F. S. Regs., Part II. and the Staff Manual respectively. Title pages will be prepared in manuscript.

WAR DIARY
or
INTELLIGENCE SUMMARY.
(Erase heading not required.)

Army Form C. 2118.

Place	Date 1918	Hour	Summary of Events and Information	Remarks and references to Appendices
IN THE LINE	Oct. 25		Battalion in billets in SWEVEGHEM. Companies standing by at half an hour's notice. Weather fine & dry.	
	26		Battalion as above. Orders received to move into Reserve area the 41st Division being relieved by 35th Division. Move off at 6 pm. Relief completed without incident. Companies all in Farms. Slight enemy aerial activity.	
	27		Battalion as above. Weather dry & mild. LIEUT. J.G. HODGE joins the Battalion & is posted to "D" Company.	
	28		Battalion as above. In celebration of the Corps Commander's Official Entry into COURTRAI, the Battalion is detailed to attend a parade held in that City representative of all arms in the Corps. The Battalion is selected to represent the 35th Division. Companies are conveyed from the line in Motor Buses to Transport Lines where they are joined by Battle Surplus & other Details, and thence march to COURTRAI, accompanied	

A7092. Wt. W128 9/M1293 750,000. 1/17. D. D & L., Ltd. Forms/C2118/14.

Instructions regarding War Diaries and Intelligence Summaries are contained in F. S. Regs., Part II. and the Staff Manual respectively. Title pages will be prepared in manuscript.

WAR DIARY
or
INTELLIGENCE SUMMARY.
(*Erase heading not required.*)

Army Form C. 2118.

Place	Date 1918	Hour	Summary of Events and Information	Remarks and references to Appendices
COURTRAI	OCT. 28		by the Massed Pipers of the 106th Infantry Brigade. The Parade is held in the GRAND PLACE where the Battalion, along with other representative troops is drawn up in column of Double Companies. The Town Band plays the Belgian & British National Anthem during which troops give the General Salute. The Corps Commander is received by the Burgomaster after which the troops march back, halting at Transport Lines for half an hours rest.	
			Massed Band of Brigade Pipers play nearly daily in COURTRAI getting much applause + approval from Civilians and Divisional & Corps Staffs, & Belgian troops.	
	29		Battalion in billets in Support to the Brigade in the Line. Are accomodated in Farms. Enemy quiet. Considerable bombing activity over back areas by enemy planes. Qr. Stores & Transport Lines move forward to village SWEVEGHEM.	

A7092. Wt. W128 9/M1293 750,000. 1/17. D. D. & L., Ltd. Forms/C2118/14

Instructions regarding War Diaries and Intelligence Summaries are contained in F. S. Regs., Part II. and the Staff Manual respectively. Title pages will be prepared in manuscript.

WAR DIARY
or
INTELLIGENCE SUMMARY.
(Erase heading not required.)

Army Form C. 2118.

Place	Date	Hour	Summary of Events and Information	Remarks and references to Appendices
	1918			
IN THE LINE	Oct 30		Battalion in Billets as above, Weather dry. Companies engaged in Field Training. Slight enemy artillery activity	
	31		Battalion as above. Artillery activity normal.	

Campbell Capt
a/Adjt for C.O.

A7092 Wt W128 9/M1293 750,000. 1/17. D. D. & L., Ltd. Forms/C2118/14.

12th Battalion Highland Light Infantry

REPORT ON OPERATIONS
27-9-18 - 1-10-18

27/9/18
10 p.m. Battalion passed starting point on Light Railway West of YPRES - KRUISTRAATE road at 10 p.m. and proceeded via DOLLS HOUSE to forming up position 100 yards West of MANOR FARM, a taping party under Lieut. Nelson having preceeded the Battalion at 7.45 p.m.
Advance to forming up point was uneventful except fot a light barrage of gas shells about DOLLS HOUSE which was passed through successfully with one casualty wounded at duty.

28/9/18
2.30 a.m. Battalion all successfully formed up on tapes by 2.30 a.m. and lay in assaulting position awaiting time for assault. There was a little intermittent shelling, but nothing serious and no casualties.

5.25 a.m. Battalion advanced to the assault in 8 waves under cover of barrage. The barrage was excellent, and the leading troops creeping well up to it carried all objectives with little difficulty. There was some slight opposition from hostile M.G's, especially in ZILLEBEKE village where a few pockets of enemy had been overrun by leading Companies, but were speedily cleared up by Supporting Companies.

6.45 a.m. About 6.45 a.m. HEDGE St. TUNNELS cleared and report to that effect forwarded to Brigde Headquarters.
The Battalion was now right up against the barrage, and had to hold back a bit to avoid casualties from it, but immediately it lifted the advance was continued, TORTOP TUNNELS and CANADA TUNNELS were passed over and the line carried forward about 500 yards East of these places.

7.30 a.m. About 7.30 a.m. all objectives being gained, and the line advanced to form a screen well East of them, I ordered the advance to cease and reorganization and consolidation to be commenced, notifying Brigade Head uarters by runner of
7.35 a.m. the situationx at 7.35 a.m.
Consolidation was slightly hampered by a few hostile snipers and M.G's. These could not be sufficiently accurately located to admit of the use of T.M's, but were soon silenced
9.15 a.m. by our Lewis Guns, and appeared to withdraw about 9.15 a.m. at about which hour the 18th Highland Light Infantry commenced to arrive and to form up West of the crest line preparatory to passing through the Battalion on their way to the second objective, ALASKA HOUSE.

9.50 a.m. At 9.50 a.m. the 18th H.L.I. passed through the Battalion and advanced on ALASKA HOUSE, 1 platoon "C" Company under Lieut. Callam, M.C. moved with the Reserve Company, 18th H.L.I. to keep touch and notify me as to progress of their advance.
Meantime/

9.50 a.m. Meantime the Battalion got properly reorganised in a defensive line about GLOSTER DRIVE, through CLONMEL COPSE and just East of DUNBARTON TRACK, liason posts being established ~~xxxxxxxx~~ on the flanks with D.L.I. on the right and Border Regt. on the left. The front was divided evenly into three, "C" Company on right, "B" Company centre and "D" Company left, each Company having three platoons front line and 1 platoon in support, "A" Company being in reserve in some old trenches about I.30.b.5.9., 1 section, 106 T.M.B. in a position of readiness about TORTOP TUNNELS, and Battalion Headquarters in HEDGES STREET TUNNELS - the 17th Royal Scots being in reserve.

During the above described phase of the operations our casualties were light, and the operation was carried out with ease and precision despite a certain difficulty experienced at the start in keeping direction owing to it being still dark, and a very wet and misty morning.

The Artillery barrage was excellent, and for an unregistered barrage, most surprisingly accurate, very few casualties being suffered from our own shells, and these mostly due to over-eagerness on the part of the infantry who had pushed right on into the danger zone.

A few of the enemy were killed ~~were~~ with rifle, Lewis Gun, revolver or bayonet during the advance, but the number captured was very much greater.

About 5 officers and 200 O.R. were captured including the Battalion Commander, also three 77 m.m. guns, 2 trench mortars, more than a dozen M.G's and large quantities of stores of ~~xxxxxxxxxxxxx~~ various sorts. The number of M.G's captured can only be very roughly estimated, as there was no time to count any booty captured West of the crest line, but 7 were taken in HEDGES STREET TUNNELS alone.

2 p.m. The day was spent in resting and refitting, Lieut Callan and his platoon returning about 2 p.m. with the information that the 18th H.L.I. had captured ALASKA HOUSE by 12.30 p.m. This platoon captured 2 prisoners while advancing with the 18th H.L.I.

<u>29/9/18</u>
5 a.m. Received orders at 5 a.m. to move up close in rear of 17th Royal Scots and 18th H.L.I. preparatory to the Brigade moving forward in support of the 105th Infantry Brigade who were about to advance on ZANDVOORDE.

6.30 a.m. Battalion moved off at 6.30 a.m. and took up a position of readiness in DELGLAN WOOD.

12.25 p.m. At 12.30 p.m. received word that 105th Infantry Brigade intended to attack the line TINBRIELAN - BLASPORT Farm at 12.30 p.m., and that the 106th Inf. Bgde. would move in support, the Battalion being in reserve about 800 yards in rear of the 17th Royal Scots and 18th H.L.I. At the same time was told not to move without orders from Brigade. One platoon "A" Company under Lieut Young was sent off at once to keep touch with the 18th H.L.I., and the remainder of the Battalion warned to be prepared to move at short notice, "C" Company on the right, "D" Company on the left, "B" Company in support and "A" Company in reserve, - No3 section "A" Company, 35th M.G.C. and 1 section 106th T.M.B. moving with Battalion Headquarters in rear of reserve Coy.

2.10 p.m.

2.10 p.m. Received orders from Brigade at 2.10 p.m. to move at once in accordance with above mentioned instructions.

2.25 p.m. Battalion moved off, "D" Company moving North of the KLEIN ZILLEBEKE - ZANVOORDE - TINERIELAN road, and the remainder South of that road.
Advanced Battalion Headquarters moved off at once ahead of the Battalion to 105th and 106th Inf. Bgdes. Headquarters at P.2.a.80.85., on arrival at which place word was received that 105th Inf. Bgde. were not advancing on ZANDVOORDE until 3 p.m. and that some of their supporting Battalions were still behind the 106th Inf. Bgde. line.

2.55 p.m. I therefore halted the Battalion sending the order by runner direct from Advanced Battalion Headquarters, and confirming by signal to Main Battalion Headquarters. The message was received alright by all except "C" Company, who had pushed on too fast, and with whom the runner failed to get touch, giving the message to an officer of another Company in error. "C" Company therefore moved striaght on South of ZANDVOORDE and came in wide on the right flank of the 17th Royal Scots who were at that time heavily engaged with the enemy between ZANDVOORDE and TINERIELAN. The enemy had a large nest of M.G's in this locality, and the advance was held up temporarily, but the arrival of this Company and the fact that the hostile M.G. crews early in their advance, appeared to cause the enemy to waver, and the advance was successfully continued to just West of TINERIELAN, where a halt was made owing to approaching darkness, though patrols sent out that night discovered that the enemy had retired right through the village.

6.15 p.m. Received orders about 6.15 p.m. for remainder of Battalion to advance again in support of 18th H.L.I. keeping North of ZAANVOORDE road.

6.20 p.m. The Battalion move off about 800 yards in rear of the 18th H.L.I. "D" Company leading, 1 section under Lieut. Aitken moving with reserve Companies 18th H.L.I. to keep touch. The remainder of the Battalion and M.C's and T.M's attached moved to the left across the road and followed in rear of "D" Company.
When darkness came on, Battn. Hqrs., Section M.G.C. and T.M.B. halted at P.2.b.9.8. and remainder of Battalion at ZAANVOORDE, at which place "C" Company rejoined the Battn. Advanced Battn. Hqrs. moved on to Hqrs. 17th Royal Scots and 18th H.L.I. at P.10.a.5.2. while the Companies reorganised, issued rations and rested where they were.

10 p.m. About 10 p.m. received orders that the advance would be continued at 6.15 a.m. 30/9/18, the Battalion moving in front line on the right of the 18th H.L.I., the 15th Cheshire Regt. being in right support and the 17th Royal Scots in left support, with view to capturing WERVICK by enveloping both flanks. Sent back for all Battn. Hqrs. all Company Commanders and officers i/c sections M.G.C. and T.M.B. attached, and on their arrival reconnoitred a jumping off place in rear of the front line roughly along the road running/

10 p.m. running through P.10.a. to Fme des OBEAUX, joining with the right of the 18th H.L.I. at that point, the right flank of the Battalion resting on the ZANDVOORDE - TINBRIELAN road.

30/9/18

1.30 a.m. Received orders 1.30 a.m. that the intention was not to envelope WERVICK, but to attack northern outskirts of the town, pushing through as far as possible at discretion of Commanding Officers.
The forming up positions being decided on, guides went back to fetch up the troops, and all was in readiness by about

4.30 a.m. except that the section M.G.C. had not yet arrived.

6.15 a.m. At 6.15 a.m. the Battalion in conjunction with the 18th H.L.I. advanced to the attack, the right Company directing, moving on a magnetic bearing of 147 degrees with their right flank resting on the ZANDVOORDE - TINBRIELAN road. "B" Company on the right, "D" Company on the left, "A" Company in support and "C" Company in reserve, the section M.G.C. not having yet arrived were ordered to follow up on arrival, and the section T.M.B. having no dry ammunition were sent to await orders at P.10.a.5.2.
Battn. H qrs. were established at Fme des OBEAUX.

6.45 a.m. At about 6.45 a.m. attack seemed progressing well, leading troops were through TINBRIELEN.
Brigadier General arrived at Battn. H rs. and Advanced Battn. Hqrs. moved off after the Battalion, coming up with it at about P.24.c.8.7. just in front of which place the advance was held up by heavy M.G. fire from the front and right flanks.
I ordered leading Company of the Cheshires to try and work round the right flank and clear out the obstructing M.G's.
Shortly after this "B" and "D" Companies who had penetrated into the outskirts of WERVICK were compelled to withdraw owing to M.G. fire from right behind their right flank.
I therefore ordered up one Company of the Cheshires to about P.24.c.central and ordered "C" Company to prepare to advance from P.24.c.8.7. due S.E. Then ordered "B" and "D" Companies to reform and "D" Company to advance on the right of the Cheshires Company, acting as right flank guard, and "B" Company get into position to move in support of "C" Company. When all were in position I ordered "C" Coy. and the Cheshire Company to advance, "D" Company to move echeloned behind the right rear of the Cheshire Company, and ½ "B" Company to move forward in support of "C" Company.
The attack progressed well to a line about P.24.d.8.4. - P.30.b.6.9. - P.30.a.95.80. - P.30.a.90.30., but was there again held up by very heavy M.G. fire, the right flank's advance again seeming to be slow and difficult.
I therefore sent another Company 15th Cheshires to try and envelope the right flank, but unfortunately it failed to get far enough round and came up and strengthened the other Company of the same Battalion in line.
The/

6.45 a.m. The 17th Royal Scots endeavoured at the same time to advance on the left flank of the 18th H.L.I., but pressing well forward almost to the outskirts of the village, were heavily engaged by hostile M.G's on their left rear and had to withdraw and swing back a defensive flank.
Seeing 17th Royal Scots withdrawing, I sent ½ section M.G.C. (who had now arrived up) to their assistance, and also placed reserve Company 15th Cheshires at disposal of O.C. 17th Royal Scots to secure his flank if necessary.
As touch could not be gained with troops on the flanks, and the M.G. fire could not be overcome by infantry and M.Guns alone, and having now only 1 Company 15th Cheshires immediately available for reserves, in conjunction with C.O's 17th Royal Scots and 18th H.L.I. it was decided to hold on where we were and not to make any further attempts to advance for the time being. This order was confirmed later by Brigade.
As it appeared possible that O.C. 17th Royal Scots might need the remaining Company 15th Cheshires to secure his left, I applied to Brigade for a direct call on another Company of the 105th Inf. Bgde. and was allotted a Company of the 15th Sherwood Foresters.

4.30 p.m. Advanced H rs. along with that of 18th H.L.I. withdrew to a pill box about P.23.b.7.0. and receiving orders that we were to continue to hold the line for the night, made all necessary arrangements for doing so.

1/10/18
7 a.m. Received orders that 7th R.I.R. would relieve the whole Brigade by daylight or dark at discretion of C.O's.
Decided that a daylight relief was inadvisable, but thinned out the line considerably, sending my "A" and "B" Companies back to Main Battn. H rs. at Fme des OISEAUX, also 30% of troops in front line. The enemy was quiet, but evidently still in position, as he opened desultry M.G. fire on any movement.

7 p.m. Guides sent to TINBRIELEN to lead in relieving troops who arrived to time, and despite some considerable hostile shelling, relief was successfully completed by 10.30 p.m., the Battalion withdrawing via TINBRIELEN to the neighbourhood of the junction of the YPRES-MENIN and KRUISEKE - BECELAERE roads.
The casualties suffered in the later phases of the operations were considerably heavier than in the first phase, although the numbers of enemy killed and captured were less. This was due in my opinion to the lack of artillery support.
The officers, N.C.O's and men all behaved with great gallantry and determination throughout, the good leadership of subordinate commanders being particularly worthy of remark.
I consider that the way the men stuck to their work during the attack on WERWICK and during the following night, was worthy of high praise, as they had been fighting already for some 24 hours, and the weather was exceptionally wet and cold/

7 p.m. and cold, so bad that there were one or two cases of men collapsing from exposure at their posts.

The Machine Gun Section attached to the Battalion worked admirably, and though they unfortunately had little opportunity of distinguishing themselves, they were always ready and keen to do all possible. I should particularly like to mention the keenness and thoroughness of Comdg. No. 3 Section, "A" Company M.G.C. who was attached to me from 23/[illegible]/18 to 30/[illegible]/18.

The rationing arrangements were excellent throughout, - at no time was the Battalion short of food or water.

I consider the Medical Officer attached to the Battalion did excellent work under very trying circumstances.

It is difficult to pick out exceptionally deserving casss from such large numbers of equally excellent material, but I forward herewith some recommendations for your approval.

Lieut. Col.
Comdg. 12th Highland L. Infantry.

12th Battalion Highland Light Infantry

NARRATIVE OF OPERATIONS
14-10-18 to 21-10-18

- - - - - - - - - - - - - - - - - -

14-10-18

5.35 hours — The Battalion moved off in Artillery Formation from K.30.c. to old front line in support of 104th and 105th Infantry Brigades. Very thick mist made the keeping of touch and direction difficult. Enemy counter barrage very scattered and few casualties suffered passing through it.

9.35 hours — Reports received from all Companies, so Brigade notified that Battalion was all in position.

13.30 hours — Battalion moved up to a position of readiness about the line of the railway in L.30.c. and L.26.a.

15-10-18

13 hours — Received orders the Brigade would either go through remainder of Division as advance guard or would be required to relieve forward troops, necessary reconnaissance carried out and details of relief arranged.

20.45 hours — Received orders that an attack would take place through front line troops, and orders would be issued at Brigade H.Qrs., FLEA CORNER 22.30 hours.

22.00 hours — Ordered Battalion to move up to a position of readiness about DARK HOUSE L.30.b.

16-10-18

00.30 hours — Reported FLEA CORNER and received orders to advance through 19th D.L.I. to the LYS, the Battalion being Left Assaulting Battalion with "A" Company 35th Battn. M.G.C. attached.

5.20 hours — Battalion all formed up in G.28.a. and 27.b. after some difficulty due to darkness and having had no time for previous reconnaissance.

5.30 hours — Battalion advanced in 4 waves on a 2 Company front behind a barrage. ½ section M.G.C. attached to each leading Company, 2 sections in reserve. The barrage was somewhat ragged and the proportion of shorts was high, no casualties however suffered from it.
No opposition met with until about 800 yards from the LYS when enemy opened heavy M.G. fire from the Eastern bank, also desultry artillery fire and some light T.M's.
It being impossible to get at the enemy owing to the river intervening, and the banks of the river being low and flat, a line was taken up about St.OMER Farm H.5.a.1.6. - G.35.d.2.2. G.35.d.7.9. - G.35.d.85.70., the left flank being thrown back to the railway in G.29.d.4.4.

9.00 hours — No further advance being practicable without preparation, line reorganised to 2 Company front, 1 Company Support and 1 Company Reserve. Battn. H.Qrs. in the Aerodrome G.34.c.4.5. ½ section M.G.C. with each front line Company, 1 section on railway line, ½ section on each flank and 1 section in reserve in G.29.a.

17-10-18.

00.10 hours Orders received to force crossing over the LYS.
1 platoon and 1 section R.E. ordered to get into a position of readiness and artillery support wired for.
Owing to short time available to organise, barrage was unable to take place, and daylight arriving nothing was accomplished.
During the day scheme arranged to force the passage of the LYS at three places M.5.c.central, M.5.b.6.8. and C.35.a.3.8., 1 section R.E. detailed to construction of each bridge, and 1 platoon to escort R.E. and form close Bridge Head East of the LYS, pending Royal Scots passing through and occupying MARCKE.

22 hours Under cover of Artillery and M.G. barrage, bridging parties advanced. Bridge at M.5.c.central could not be constructed owing to magnitude of the bridging operation entailed and strong enemy opposition. Bridge at M.5.b.6.8 thrown across successfully and bridgehead established East of the LYS. Work commenced on bridge at C.36.a.3.8. and about 30 feet constructed, then 2 enemy M.Gs brought up close to Eastern bank, and heavy enemy shelling, chiefly gas, prevented further work.
R.E. parties and escorting platoons of 2 flank bridges withdrawn, posts being established close to Western bank of LYS and bridgehead platoon on centre bridge relieved, 2 platoons of Royal Scots passing through to raid and ascertain situation on the Eastern bank, orders having been received that an extended bridgehead was not desired.

18/10/18.

07.00 hours Mist which had been thick lifting, and position East of Canal being bad, owing to lack of cover and wet state of ground, post withdrawn to cover bridge from West bank.

22.30 hours After artillery preparation, pontoon bridges thrown over the river at M.5.b.6.8. and C.36.a.3.8. "A" Company plus 1 section 106th T.M.B. passing over the light bridge constructed the previous night to cover the operation, 1 platoon escorting R.E. party working on bridge at C.36.a.3.8. and passing over it when constructed, joining with left of "A" Company, on the line of the MARCKEBEEKE in C.36.a. 4 4.

19/10/18.

04.00 hours 104th Infantry Brigade passed through at 4 a.m. and Battalion closed to position of readiness in and about BISSEGHEM. Battalion moved to billets in MARCKE.

20/10/18.

07.00 hours Moved off from MARCKE in column of route, Brigade being in reserve to 104th and 105th Infantry Brigades, halting in positions of readiness about HOOGHE (P.3.c.)

18.00 hours Received orders to move up to right of 104th Infantry Brigade about N.35 and clear the ridge from there to Q.31.central.

19.15 hours Having ascertained situation Battalion moved off from N.35.central to make flank attack along ridge towards HOOGSTRAATE, "D", "C" and "A" Companies, Battalion Headquarters and 2½ sections "C" Company M.G.C. moving in advance guard formation along road I.5.b.3.4. -

19.15 hours (Continued)
- N.36.d.5.3. - O.31.b.1.5.
"B" Company with ½ section M.G.C. moving along parallel load N.35.d.1.5 - N.30.b.9.9. - O.25.c.7.4., "D" Company 18th H.L.I. following the main part of the Battalion to establish posts in rear of the Battalion as it passed clear of front line.

21.00 hours. Head of Battalion held up by M.G. fire from MOLEN le CLAERC. Remainder of the Battalion cleared off the road into defensive positions about Cross Roads O.31.b.3.5. with Battalion Headquarters at Cross roads, while leading Company ("D" Company) advanced to try and clear high ground about MOLEN le CLAERC. Patrol sent off to get touch with "B" Company on left flank.

23.30 hours "D" Company having met strong wire obstacle, with M.Gs. behind it determined to swing left flank, ask for shelling of MOLEN le CLAERC and send forward to make it good on shelling ceasing at 02.03 hours. Touch gained with "B" Company who were similarly situated and with Headquarters 18th H.L.I. at O.25.c.7.4.
Disposed Battalion on line O.31.b.2.4. - O.25.c.9.5. - O.26.a.7.3. - N.24.d.7.3. Headquarters O.24.d.3.2.
Situation as regards enemy difficult to ascertain as M.G. fire and sniping appeared to come from any direction though several farms from which fire appeared to come when searched, were found to contain no enemy, the inhabitants saying that they had just left.

21/10/18.
03.30 hours Received word from right Company enemy still in occupation MOLEN le CLAERC, but his patrols still trying to work round them.

04.50 hours Received word from Right Company that MOLEN le CLAERC clear of enemy and touch gained there with Right of 17th Royal Scots.

07.00 hours 41st Division passed through.

12.00 hours Battalion marched back to billets S.E. of COURTRAY.

Total casualties during period :- Officers - 2 wounded.
O.R. - 4 killed.
- 41 wounded.
- 7 unaccounted for.

Total captures during period :- 1 prisoner.
2 heavy M.Gs.
1 light M.G.

I consider that all ranks worked hard and did their best during an extended period of continual effort and little rest. The fighting was at no time very heavy as the enemy when met in the open wasted no time in getting away, while, on other occasions, obstacles prevented our getting to close quarters with him. The outstanding lessons learned during these operations were the need for a great improvement in section leading and initiative of junior N.C.Os, particularly as regards getting men quickly shaken out from close formations when coming under close fire, and as regards selection of fire positions and principles of fire and movement and the fact that the Lewis Gun and bayonet have so far become the infantry weapons that the use of the rifle requires a considerable amount of training in open warfare before being developed to anywhere near the extent desirable

Lieut.-Colonel.
Commdg. 12th Battalion Highland Light Infantry.

Instructions regarding War Diaries and Intelligence Summaries are contained in F. S. Regs., Part II. and the Staff Manual respectively. Title pages will be prepared in manuscript.

WAR DIARY
or
~~INTELLIGENCE SUMMARY.~~
(Erase heading not required.)

12th Bn H.L.I.

November 1918

Army Form C. 2118.

Place	Date	Hour	Summary of Events and Information	Remarks and references to Appendices
IN RESERVE KNOCKE	1918 Nov.r 1		Battalion in Billets in & around KNOCKE. Intermittent shelling throughout the days particularly of roads & railways & villages. Weather dry & cold	
BELLEGHEM	2		Battalion move by March Route to vicinity of BELLEGHEM & are billeted in the village & outskirts. Considerable activity of enemy planes during the course of the night. Main traffic routes & villages behind the line being heavily bombed.	
	3		Battalion in billets as above. Draft of 48 O.R. join the Battalion.	
	4		do 2/LIEUT. D. GRANT joins the Battn.	
	5		do 2/LIEUT. F.B. FOSTER, & 2/LIEUT. J. ANDERSON join the Battalion. Battalion moves by march route via HOOGE to COURTRAI, where A, B, & D Companies are billeted together & "C" Company at the Station. Billets good & plenty accomodation. Warning Order received to be ready to move in the event of the enemy withdrawing.	
	6		Battalion billeted as above. Draft of 7 O.R. received.	

A7092 Wt W128 9/M1293 750,000 1/17 D. D & L., Ltd. Forms/C2118/14.

Instructions regarding War Diaries and Intelligence Summaries are contained in F. S. Regs., Part II. and the Staff Manual respectively. Title pages will be prepared in manuscript.

WAR DIARY
or
INTELLIGENCE SUMMARY.
(Erase heading not required.)

Army Form C. 2118.

Place	Date	Hour	Summary of Events and Information	Remarks and references to Appendices
COURTRAI	1918 Novr. 7		Battalion in billets as above. LIEUT. H.S.D. SMITH rejoins the Battalion & is given command of 'C' Company.	
	8		Battalion in billets as above. Draft of 7 O.R. received. LIEUT. J.W. HAWLEY is transferred to Signal Service R.E.	
	9		Battalion move forward to TIEGHEM with a view to following up retreating enemy. Billets very poor & cramped. Weather dry & cold.	
	10		Battalion move by march route & cross the SCHELDT, arriving at SULSIQUE.	
	11		Battalion move at 9.40 A.M. & proceed to LEYNSTRAAT by march route. About 10.40 A.M. the Divisional Commander passed in his car & conveyed the news that the armistice was expected to come into operation at 11 A.M. The news received very quietly by the men who were not inclined to believe it until the cessation of gun-fire actually took place.	

A7092. Wt W128 9/M1293 750,000. 1/17. D. D & L., Ltd. Forms/C2118/14.

Army Form C. 2118.

Instructions regarding War Diaries and Intelligence Summaries are contained in F. S. Regs., Part II. and the Staff Manual respectively. Title pages will be prepared in manuscript.

WAR DIARY
or
INTELLIGENCE SUMMARY.
(Erase heading not required.)

Place	Date	Hour	Summary of Events and Information	Remarks and references to Appendices
LEYNSTRAAT	1918 Nov. 11		LEYNSTRAAT is reached about 3.30 p.m. & the Companies proceed to billets in the village.	
	12		Battalion in billets as above. Weather dry & cold. French [illegible] prevails & the last of prisoners taken by our men pass through the village, consisting of a few men & one officer having his face considerably knocked about. The first batch of our released prisoners pass through the village & are given a welcome by our men.	
	13		Battalion moves back close to NUKERKE, arrive after dark & have to wait till the 41st Division move out of billets. Weather dry & very cold, keen frost prevailing.	
	14		Battalion as above. Men rest & clean up. Draft of 5 or. received.	
	15		Battalion as above. A good football ground adjoining is taken advantage of as far as the number of footballs permit.	

A7092. Wt. W128 9/M1293 750,000. 1/17. D. D. & L., Ltd. Forms/C2118/14.

Army Form C. 2118.

Instructions regarding War Diaries and Intelligence Summaries are contained in F. S. Regs., Part II, and the Staff Manual respectively. Title pages will be prepared in manuscript.

WAR DIARY
or
INTELLIGENCE SUMMARY.
(Erase heading not required.)

Place	Date	Hour	Summary of Events and Information	Remarks and references to Appendices
	1918			
NUKERKE	NOV.R 16		Battalion as above.	
	17		do	
	18		Battalion moves to HARLEBEEKE by march route, staging one night at INGOYGHEM. Men without blankets were very cold &	
	19		billets were very draughty & poor.	
HARLEBEEKE	20		Battalion arrive in HARLEBEEKE. Blankets & packs drawn & men are accomodated in good & commodious billets. Weather dry & cold. LIEUT. C. WALKER joins the Battalion. Draft of 13 O.R. received.	
	21		Battalion as above.	
	22		Ditto	
	23		Ditto Draft of 7 O.R. arrived. LIEUT. W. S. WILSON reports to the Battalion for duty.	
	24		Battalion as above. Weather clear & cold	
	25		do	
	26		do	

A7092. Wt. W128 9/M1293 750,000. 1/17. D. D. & L., Ltd. Forms/C2118/14.

Army Form C. 2118.

Instructions regarding War Diaries and Intelligence Summaries are contained in F. S. Regs., Part II. and the Staff Manual respectively. Title pages will be prepared in manuscript.

WAR DIARY
or
INTELLIGENCE SUMMARY.

(Erase heading not required.)

Place	Date	Hour	Summary of Events and Information	Remarks and references to Appendices
	1918			
HARLEBEKE	NOV. 26		Battalion moves by march route to MENIN, & are billeted there in the College	
	27		Battalion move by march Route to YPRES. Weather very wet. Companies are accomodated in the BARRACKS & Head Quarters in the Ramparts.	
	28		Battalion move to ABEELE & are billeted in the village.	
	29		Battalion move to WULVERDINGHE & are billeted over night.	
	30		Battalion move by March Route to HOULLE and are billeted in the village & surrounding area. Billets very poor & very scattered.	

[signature] Campbell Capt.
A/Adjt. for C.O.

A7092 Wt W128 9/M1293 750,000 1/17. D. D & L., Ltd. Forms/C2118/14.

12TH HIGHLAND LIGHT INFANTRY.

FIGHTING STRENGH (Officers.) Week Ending 29-11-18.

Command.	2ND in Command.	No. of Majors and Captains	No. of Subalterns.	Total.
Lieut-Col. J.N.O. Rycroft, D.S.O., M.C.	Capt. J. Houston	6	38	46.

29-11-18.

Capt. & Adjt.
for O.C. 12th H.L.I.

12th HIGHLAND LIGHT INFANTRY.

Increase and Decrease to Strength. Week Ending 30-11-1918.

Increase.	Officers.	Lieut. A. Anderson.	Joined Battalion	26-11-18.
		Lieut. W. Gordon.	do.	26-11-18.
		2/Lt. W. S. Kerr.	do.	26-11-18.
		" D. McGirr.	do.	26-11-18.
		" G. A. Swann.	do.	26-11-18.
		" J. W. Main.	do.	26-11-18.
		1 Lieut. R. B. Aitken, M.C.	do. (from Hospital)	26-11-18.
	O.R.	11 O.R. Joined Battalion 23-11-18.		
		4 O.R. " " 25-11-18.		
		15		
Decrease.	Officers.	2/Lt. J. M. Clements to U.K. and struck off strength 23-11-18. (Interpreter to B.E.F. Nth Russia). (Auth:- 1st Echelon D.A.A.G. 6192(0) d/12-11-18.	O.R. :- 17. O.R. transferred to C.C.S. (Sick) 23-11-18 to 26-11-18.	

29-11-18.

Capt. & Adjt.
for O.C. 12th H.L.I.

STRENGH RETURN.

Made up to Noon 30th No

UNIT.	Column I. Fighting Strengh for Previous Week.		Column II. Increase During Week Due to Drafts etc.		Column III. Total from I and II		Column IV. Decrease During Week Due to Casualties, etc.		Column A. FIGHTING STRENGH.		Column B. Not with Battalion and not at disposal of C.O.		A Minus B Available. Fighting Strengh.	
	Off.	O.R.	Off.	O.R.	Off.	O.R.	Off.	O.R.	Off	O.R.	Off.	O.R.	Off.	O.R.
12th H.L.I.	40	776	7	15	47	791	1	17	46	774	6	154	40	620

Capt. & Adjt.
for O.C. 12th Bn. High. L.I.

COLUMN "B"

	Off.	O.R.
(A) H.Q. 106th I.B.		
Orderlies	–	7
Officer's Servt	–	1
Mess Waiter.	–	1
Draughtsman.	–	1
Assistant to P.T. B.T. Instructor	–	1
Armourer's Asst	–	1
(B) H.Q. 35th Division.		
Signals,	–	3
Observation Group,	–	1
Divisional Guard.	–	11
(C) Officers & O.R. in F.A.	–	17.
(D) Officers in F.A. not yet reported invalided home.	3	–
(E) Officers and O.R. attached to T.M. Batteries.	–	5
(F) Officers and O.R. employed at Schools. 35th Div. Signals School.	–	1
XIX Corps Infantry School.	–	11
Officers and O.R. attending Courses.	1	10
(G) 35th Div. Baths.	1	1
A.C.G. IV Army	–	1
18th H.L.I.	–	1
A.S.C. (Div. Train)	–	2
(H) On Leave.	1	78
	6	154

Instructions regarding War Diaries and Intelligence Summaries are contained in F. S. Regs., Part II. and the Staff Manual respectively. Title pages will be prepared in manuscript.

WAR DIARY or INTELLIGENCE SUMMARY.

(Erase heading not required.)

Army Form C. 2118.

12 HLI

37

Place	Date	Hour	Summary of Events and Information	Remarks and references to Appendices
WULVERDINGHE	1918 DEC. 1		Battalion in billets in WULVERDINGHE AREA. Move by March Route to HOULLE arriving about 1 pm.	
HOULLE	2		Battalion in billets in HOULLE. Accomodation very poor & billets widely scattered. Intimation received that the Military Cross is awarded to 2/LIEUT. D.J. REOCH, Battalion Transport Officer for Gallantry & Devotion to Duty.	
	3		Battalion in Billets as above. Web equipment in possession of men in the Battalion changed for equipment of Leather pattern, so as to ensure conformity in the Battalion.	
	4		Battalion in Billets as above. Companies carry out elementary training & short route marches.	
	5		Battalion in Billets as above. Strong representations made to Brigade as to inadequacy & the discomfort of the Men's billets.	
	6		Battalion as above. Orders received to move to MILLAM, & move by March Route completed by 3.30 p.m.	
MILLAM	7		Battalion settled in Hutted Camp which proves in spite of	

A5834 Wt. W4973/M687 750,000 8/16 D. D. & L. Ltd. Forms/C.2118/13

Army Form C. 2118.

Instructions regarding War Diaries and Intelligence Summaries are contained in F. S. Regs., Part II. and the Staff Manual respectively. Title pages will be prepared in manuscript.

WAR DIARY
or
INTELLIGENCE SUMMARY.
(Erase heading not required.)

Place.	Date	Hour	Summary of Events and Information	Remarks and references to Appendices
	1918			
MILLAM	DEC 7		of lack of Camp furniture, a great improvement on previous accomodation.	
			The following decorations have been approved & made by the French Authorities to Officers & men of the Battalion:-	
			CROIX DE GUERRE DE L'ORDRE DE DIVISION, 839 Pte. A.T. QUEEN	
			do DE BRIGADE, LIEUT. A.L. BRYSON	
			do DE REGIMENT, 7749, PTE. C. HANNAN	
	8		Battalion in Hutted Camp. Parade Church Service held in MILLAM VILLAGE	
	9		Battalion as above. Education Classes formed under supervision of LIEUT. W.M. CLOW, 2/LIEUT. S. McGIRR & ALLAN being detailed to assist.	
	10		Battalion as above. Musketry for two Companies carried out under CAPT. S. CAMPBELL, M.C. on WATTEN RANGE, for one Company on MILLAM RANGE under LIEUT. J. ROBERTSON, M.C.; 30 O.R. (coal-miners) despatched for Demobilization	[signature]
	11		Battalion as above. Mess Meeting held to discuss proposal to form a Battalion Officers Mess.	

A5834 Wt. W4973/M687 750,000 8/16 D. D. & L. Ltd. Forms/C.2118/13

Instructions regarding War Diaries and Intelligence Summaries are contained in F. S. Regs., Part II. and the Staff Manual respectively. Title pages will be prepared in manuscript.

WAR DIARY
or
INTELLIGENCE SUMMARY.
(Erase heading not required.)

Army Form C. 2118.

Place.	Date	Hour	Summary of Events and Information	Remarks and references to Appendices
MILLAM	1918 DEC. 12		Battalion as above. Short parades carried out under Company arrangement consisting principally of Physical Training, Musketry & Squad Drill, the afternoon being devoted to Recreational Training. A riding class for Officers is formed to which four Officers are sent daily. Party of 5 O.R. dispatched for Demobilization as Miners.	
	13		Battalion as above. Battalion parades commenced forming in Mass in field in neighbourhood of the Camp. Subsequent parades carried on under Company arrangements. All men attending Education Classes are exempted from Company parades. Intimation received that the more severe restrictions in regard to Sketching & the use of Cameras are relaxed.	
	14		Battalion as above. The Brigade parade in MILLAM VILLAGE to attend Ceremonial Parade for the presentation of ribands by the Divisional Commander. 4 O.R. dispatched for Demobilization as Coal Miners & Pivotal Men.	[illegible]

A5834 Wt. W4973/M687 750,000 8/16 D. D. & L. Ltd. Forms/C.2118/13

Instructions regarding War Diaries and Intelligence Summaries are contained in F. S. Regs., Part II. and the Staff Manual respectively. Title pages will be prepared in manuscript.

WAR DIARY
or
INTELLIGENCE SUMMARY.
(Erase heading not required.)

Army Form C. 2118.

Place.	Date	Hour	Summary of Events and Information	Remarks and references to Appendices
MILLAM	1918 DEC. 15		Battalion as above. Weather broken & very changeable.	
	16		do do	
	17		do The Battalion is ordered in conjunction with the two other Battalions in the Brigade to fill in system of trenches about three kilos from Camp. Trench timber & duckboards are salved & brought back to Camp, timber for fire wood & the duckboards being used to improve approaches to the Camp & Quarters of Officers and Men.	
	18		Battalion as above, engaged in filling in trenches from 9.30 a.m. to 12.30 p.m.	
	19		do do	
	20		do do First of the Ties for Divisional Football Competition in	[signature]

A5834 Wt. W4973/M687 750,000 8/16 D. D. & L. Ltd. Forms/C.2118/13

Instructions regarding War Diaries and Intelligence Summaries are contained in F. S. Regs., Part II. and the Staff Manual respectively. Title pages will be prepared in manuscript.

WAR DIARY
or
INTELLIGENCE SUMMARY.
(Erase heading not required.)

Army Form C. 2118.

Place.	Date	Hour	Summary of Events and Information	Remarks and references to Appendices
	1919			
MILLAM	DEC. 20		which the Battalion was beaten by the R.A.M.C. by three goals to nothing.	
	21		Battalion as above engaged in filling in trenches. First trip by Motor Lorry to CALAIS to which 2 Officers & 21 O.R. ~~of~~ the Battalion are given the opportunity of proceeding.	
	22		Battalion as above. Church parade held in HANGAR in village.	
	23		do Companies engage in filling in trenches & salving firewood. Weather stormy & wet.	
	24		Battalion as above. Filling in of trenches cancelled owing to wet weather. Lectures given in Camp to the men by LIEUT. W. M. CLOW & Company Commanders.	
	25		Battalion as above. Xmas day wet & cold. Men got special Rations & Free Issue of Beer. ~~[illegible]~~	[signature] Capt.
	26		Battalion as above. Trench filling suspended owing to condition of the weather & ground.	

A5834 Wt. W4973/M687 750,000 8/16 D. D. & L. Ltd. Forms/C.2118/13

Instructions regarding War Diaries and Intelligence Summaries are contained in F. S. Regs., Part II. and the Staff Manual respectively. Title pages will be prepared in manuscript.

WAR DIARY
or
INTELLIGENCE SUMMARY.
(*Erase heading not required.*)

Army Form C. 2118.

Place	Date	Hour	Summary of Events and Information	Remarks and references to Appendices
	1918			
MILLAM	DEC. 27		Battalion in hutments as above. Weather very wet & stormy & trench filling impossible owing to condition of ground. First Round in the Divisional Rugby Competition held, ending in a draw with the Northumberland Fusiliers. 30 O.R. proceed to England for Demobilization as Coal Miners.	
	28		Battalion as above, confined to Camp through bad weather. Preparations for the Mens New Year dinner taken in hand & pushed on as far as possible.	
	29		Battalion as above. Church parade in the morning in the village attended by the G.O.C. Division. Pigs slaughtered for Mens New Year Dinner and Dining Rooms fitted with tables & benches. Preparations made to start Battalion Officers Mess on New Years Day commencing with a special dinner on the evening of 31st Dec. Sergeants Mess opened in Camp.	[signature]

A5834 Wt. W4973/M687 750,000 8/16 D. D. & L. Ltd. Forms/C.2118/13

Instructions regarding War Diaries and Intelligence Summaries are contained in F. S. Regs., Part II. and the Staff Manual respectively. Title pages will be prepared in manuscript.

WAR DIARY
or
INTELLIGENCE SUMMARY.
(Erase heading not required.)

Army Form C. 2118.

Place	Date	Hour	Summary of Events and Information	Remarks and references to Appendices
MILLAM	1918 DEC. 30		Battalion in billets as above. No further trench filling possible owing to weather.	
	31		ditto Companies engaged in filling in trenches from 9.30 A.M. to 12.30 pm.	

J. H. Carter Thomas, Capt
ADJT 12 HLI.

35

Instructions regarding War Diaries and Intelligence Summaries are contained in F. S. Regs., Part II. and the Staff Manual respectively. Title pages will be prepared in manuscript.

WAR DIARY
or
INTELLIGENCE SUMMARY.
(Erase heading not required.)

12 HLI

98 38

Army Form C. 2118.

Place	Date	Hour	Summary of Events and Information	Remarks and references to Appendices
Millam	1/1/19		Battalion still encamped at Millam New Years dinner given to the men weather fair	
"	2/1/19		do do do do Trench filling weather unsettled	
	3/1/19		do do do do do do do do	
	4/1/19		do do do do do do do do	
	5/1/19		do do do do Church Parades do do	
	6/1/19		do do do do Training Musketry do do do	
	7/1/19		do do do do Trench filling weather wet	
	8/1/19		do do do do do do do do Semi final Divisional Rugby football Cup 12th HLI Nil 18th Lancashire Fusiliers Nil	
	9/1/19		do do do do Training weather unsettled	
	10/1/19		do do do do do do do	
	11/1/19		do do do do do do do	
	12/1/19		do do do do do Church Parades do do	
	13/1/19		do do do do Training do do	

A5834 Wt. W4973/M687 750,000 8/16 D. D. & L. Ltd. Forms/C.2118/13

38.M
[illegible]

Instructions regarding War Diaries and Intelligence Summaries are contained in F. S. Regs., Part II. and the Staff Manual respectively. Title pages will be prepared in manuscript.

WAR DIARY
or
INTELLIGENCE SUMMARY.
(Erase heading not required.)

Army Form C. 2118.

Place	Date	Hour	Summary of Events and Information	Remarks and references to Appendices
MILLAM	14/1/19		Battalion still encamped at MILLAM. Training weather wet	
do	15/1/19		do do do Trench filling weather unsettled.	
do	16/1/19		do do do Training do do	
do	17/1/19		do do do do weather fine	
do	18/1/19		do do do Trench filling do do	
	19/1/19		do do Church Parades weather colder.	
	20/1/19		do do Training do do replay semi final Divisional Rugby Cup 12th H L I Nil 18th Lancashire Fusiliers 3 points	
	21/1/19		do do do Training weather frosty	
	22/1/19		do do do Trench filling do do	
	23/1/19		do do do Brigade route March weather cold & frosty	[illegible]

A5834 Wt. W4973/M687 750,000 8/16 D. D. & L. Ltd. Forms/C.2118/13

Instructions regarding War Diaries and Intelligence Summaries are contained in F. S. Regs., Part II. and the Staff Manual respectively. Title pages will be prepared in manuscript.

WAR DIARY
or
INTELLIGENCE SUMMARY.
(Erase heading not required.)

Army Form C. 2118.

Place	Date	Hour	Summary of Events and Information	Remarks and references to Appendices
MILLAM	24/1/19		Battalion still encamped at MILLAM. Trench filling. weather very cold & frosty	
"	25/1/19		do do do do do do	
	26/1/19		do do do Church Parades do do	
	27/1/19		do do do Trench filling do do	
	28/1/19		do do do Divisional Rifle meeting cancelled do do	
	29/1/19		do do do Battalion moved to Calais via March route to Watten entraining there at 9 am. Train proceeded to Calais & from there went on to Dunkirk where a delay of about two hours occurred. Train then moved back to CALAIS & on arriving at DUNES STATION the Battalion detrained in conjunction with the remainder of the Brigade. The Battalion marched to No 6 Rest Camp West where the men were accommodated in tents	
CALAIS	30/1/19		Orders received to proceed to take up a line from Canal along road extending between Stations and the Strikers. Order to fix bayonets given at 11 AM. About 11 30 am large parties of strikers were observed marching down road along side Canal towards the	[illegible]

A5834 Wt. W4973/M687 750,000 8/16 D. D. & L. Ltd. Forms/C.2118/13

Instructions regarding War Diaries and Intelligence Summaries are contained in F. S. Regs., Part II. and the Staff Manual respectively. Title pages will be prepared in manuscript.

WAR DIARY
or
INTELLIGENCE SUMMARY.
(*Erase heading not required.*)

Army Form C. 2118.

Place	Date	Hour	Summary of Events and Information	Remarks and references to Appendices
CALAIS	30/1/19		CONTINUED the left flank of our line. As the strikers were peaceably inclined they were passed on by the Picquets to the CAMP at which all the Strikers were to concentrate. Cease fire [illegible] at 12 30 pm and the Battalion formed up and marched back to Camp	
	31/1/19		Battalion in Camp at [illegible]. The Battalion take part in Brigade route march through the streets of CALAIS Population being duly impressed with the fine bearing of the troops. Letter of congratulation received from General Byng Commanding troops at CALAIS	
			Number of men demobilized during month 169.	
			" Officers " 4.	
			AWARDS BELGIAN CROIX DE GUERRE Lieut-Col. J.H.O. RYCROFT. DSO MC T/CAPT. A. GILCHRIST. LIEUT O.V. HARLAND No 41125 Sgt G. SMITH " 17579 Cpl P. SULLIVAN.	

[illegible] Campbell Capt.
A/Adj for C.O.

A5834 Wt. W4973/M687 750,000 8/16 D. D. & L. Ltd. Forms/C.2118/13

Instructions regarding War Diaries and Intelligence Summaries are contained in F. S. Regs., Part II. and the Staff Manual respectively. Title pages will be prepared in manuscript.

WAR DIARY
or
~~INTELLIGENCE SUMMARY.~~
(Erase heading not required.)

From 1st to 28th Feb: 1919

12th Bn HIGHLAND L.I.

Army Form C. 2118.

39

Place	Date	Hour	Summary of Events and Information	Remarks and references to Appendices
Millam	Feb 1st	0930	Entrained at Dune Siding, Calais, for return journey to Millam.	
		1400	Detrained at Watten-Eperlecques Station and marched into Camp at Millam at 1530 hours.	
	Feb 2	0900	Battalion on wood salving.	
			The battalion has today been ordered to pay a large claim amounting to 720 francs, or about £28, on account of woodwork destroyed by troops of this battalion in a billet at HOULLE. This claim has been paid by cheque from the Regimental Canteen Funds.	
	Feb 3		Battalion parade as per D.ment. Owing to severity of weather, baths are not available. 2/Lt McGIRR D takes over temporarily charge of Battalion Education pending return of 2/Lt ALLAN J.E. 2/Lt GRAY J takes over duties of Battalion Recreational Officer pending return of Lt CALLAN J MC.	
			Special Orders. The Major General wishes to express his appreciation of the smart and soldierly manner in which all ranks of the 104, 105, & 106 Infantry Brigades, Machine Gun Battn, R.A.M.C, R.A.S.C. and Signals have carried out their duties during the past four days. Officers and men have	

2353 Wt. W2544/1454 700,000 5/15 D. D. & L. A.D.S.S./Forms/C. 2118.

39.M. 6 sheet

Instructions regarding War Diaries and Intelligence Summaries are contained in F. S. Regs., Part II. and the Staff Manual respectively. Title pages will be prepared in manuscript.

WAR DIARY

~~or~~

~~INTELLIGENCE SUMMARY.~~

(Erase heading not required.)

Army Form C. 2118.

Place	Date	Hour	Summary of Events and Information	Remarks and references to Appendices
Millam	Feb 3		shown tact and zeal and the good discipline of the Division has been particularly ~~[illegible]~~ noted. Gen. Sir Julian Byng K.C.B. K.C.M.G. M.V.O. commanding 3rd Army and temporarily troops at Calais, has told the Divisional Commander that he has reported to the C in C. in the highest terms on the Div and wishes all ranks to be informed of his satisfaction with what they have done.	
			A lecture on 'Re-enlistment in the Army of Occupation as laid down in Circular letter G.A. 619 was given under Company arrangements.	
	Feb 4.		Field Service postcards discontinued.	
	Feb 5 } 6.7. }		Battalion on wood salving.	
	Feb 8.		Battalion ~~[illegible] two Companies~~ ordered to proceed to Calais. Detachment of 3 Officers 3 Sgts and 126 other ranks proceeded to BEAUVES ~~for~~ on train guard duty, under the command of Capt. H.S.D. SMITH.	
	9.		Battalion at Calais to re-organize leave traffic.	
	10.		Entrained at 1400 hours at Dunes Siding and arrived back at Millam at 2115 hours.	W.J.

2353 Wt. W2544/1454 700,000 5/15 D. D. & L. A.D.S.S./Forms/C. 2118.

Instructions regarding War Diaries and Intelligence Summaries are contained in F. S. Regs., Part II. and the Staff Manual respectively. Title pages will be prepared in manuscript.

WAR DIARY
or
~~INTELLIGENCE~~ SUMMARY.
(Erase heading not required.)

Army Form C. 2118.

Place	Date	Hour	Summary of Events and Information	Remarks and references to Appendices
Millam	Feb 11 – 12 – 13		Battalion on wood salving. Weather Cold and dry. do.	
	14		A lecture on 'Bolshevism' delivered to battalion. & Officers – The following extracts from list No 225 of Appointments, Commissions etc dated 2 February 1919 is published for information:– Temp. Lieut H S D Smith to be A/Capt. whilst in command of a Coy. 14th Oct. 1918. The undermentioned to be A/Capt. (Additional) Temp. Lt. A. L. Bryson, 15th Oct. 1918. Lt. R. B. Aitken M.C. Lanark Yeomanry 16th Oct. 1918	
	15.		~~No Church parade~~. Wood Salving. Cold and blustery morning with heavy rain during afternoon.	
	16.		No Church parade.	
	17		Battalion on wood salving. Weather dull and heavy showers of rain impede work. Weather improves in afternoon. Battalion football team beats 108 T.M. Battery by 5 goals to nil in Brigade League	
	18.		Camp Inspection carried out by Commanding Officer. Battalion reduced	WM

2353 Wt. W2544/1454 700,000 5/15 D. D. & L. A.D.S.S./Forms/C. 2118.

Instructions regarding War Diaries and Intelligence Summaries are contained in F. S. Regs., Part II. and the Staff Manual respectively. Title pages will be prepared in manuscript.

WAR DIARY
or
~~INTELLIGENCE SUMMARY.~~
(Erase heading not required.)

Army Form C. 2118.

Place	Date	Hour	Summary of Events and Information	Remarks and references to Appendices
Millam	Feb 18		to two Companies — B Coy combined with A Coy under the command of Capt Gilchrist with Lt Anderson as second in command. D Coy combined with C Coy under the command of Capt Smith with Capt Arthur MC as second in command. Each of the new combined Companies, known as "A" and "C" Coys respectively, will consist of four platoons.	
	19.		A lecture given to Battalion by Mr W. Calderwood, Inspector of Salmon Fisheries, Scotland in Theatre at Merkeghem.	
			2/Lt Allen is appointed Battalion Educational Officer from todays date vice Lt W. S. Wilson (to hospital)	
			Battalion on wood sawing. Bright crisp weather.	
	20		do	
	21.		Battalion at baths all forenoon. Battalion team played Devon Machine Gun Battalion at Merkeghem in Brigade League, the game being a most one-sided one. We won easily by 9 goals to 1.	
	22		Battalion on rehearsal parade for Consecration of Colours.	WL

2353 Wt. W2544/1454 700,000 5/15 D. D. & L. A.D.S.S./Forms/C. 2118.

Instructions regarding War Diaries and Intelligence Summaries are contained in F. S. Regs., Part II. and the Staff Manual respectively. Title pages will be prepared in manuscript.

WAR DIARY
or
~~INTELLIGENCE SUMMARY.~~

(Erase heading not required.)

Army Form C. 2118.

Place	Date	Hour	Summary of Events and Information	Remarks and references to Appendices
Millam	Feb 23		A very imposing ceremony was witnessed today in the Hanger, Millam, the occasion being the Consecration of the battalion colours. After a short, imposing service in which the best known hymns and psalms were sung, the Chaplain handed over the items of office to Major J. Houston, who, as senior Major, handed over the colours to Major-General A.H. Marindin D.S.O., Comdg 35th Division. General Marindin paid a very glowing tribute to the battalion and briefly expounded its wonderful war record, which, the General stated, "Bravely upholds the glorious traditions of the Regiment." Lt. A. Anderson received the colours on behalf of the battalion and after a most impressive and smart march past, the colours were escorted to, and handed over to the officers mess.	
	24		Officers - 2/Lt J. E. Allan will be Act Captain whilst acting as Brigade Education Officer with effect from 22/2/19	
			Battalion on wood salving	
	25		do	

A5834 Wt. W4973/M687 750,000 8/16 D. D. & L. Ltd. Forms/C.2118/13

Instructions regarding War Diaries and Intelligence Summaries are contained in F. S. Regs., Part II. and the Staff Manual respectively. Title pages will be prepared in manuscript.

WAR DIARY
or
~~INTELLIGENCE~~ SUMMARY.
(Erase heading not required.)

Army Form C. 2118.

Place	Date	Hour	Summary of Events and Information	Remarks and references to Appendices
Millam	Feb 26		Battalion on wood sawing Weather cold and dry.	
	27		Usual parades and camp duties. The Battalion football team claim another runaway victory, their victims on this occasion being the 105 Field Ambulance who were soundly trounced to the tune of 8 goals to nil. The team, on their present form will be difficult to beat, and since the Brigade Group League started, they have only lost one game – and that by the narrow margin of 2 goals to 1 goal. – They have won all games during the month of February and have scored 22 goals and only lost 1 goal.	
	28			

A Campbell Capt.
a/Adjt for CO.

A5834 Wt. W4973/M687 750,000 8/16 D. D. & L. Ltd. Forms/C.2118/13

35th

April 1919

WAR DIARY
or
INTELLIGENCE SUMMARY.
(Erase heading not required.)

12th H. L. Infy

Army Form C. 2118.

Instructions regarding War Diaries and Intelligence Summaries are contained in F. S. Regs., Part II. and the Staff Manual respectively. Title pages will be prepared in manuscript.

Place	Date 1919	Hour	Summary of Events and Information	Remarks and references to Appendices
MILLAM	1/10th		Battalion in Camp. Demobilization of the few remaining men carried out, previous to reduction to Cadre. All Officers of the Battalion, having been demobilized or transferred to the 10th Scottish Rifles, there only remain with the Unit the Commanding Officer, Adjutant, Quarter-Master, & Lewis Gun Officer with the Chaplain.	
TILQUES	11		Cadre moves to TILQUES by Route March via WATTEN distance about 14 KILOS.	
	12/16		Cadre in hutment Camp at TILQUES	
	17		Cadre move to ST OMER entraining at 16.00 hours & arriving at DUNKIRK about 19.00 hours, where the ~~Batt~~ Cadre were accomodated in HOSPICE CAMP. Draft of 6 O.R. transferred to 10 Scottish Rifles under command of Lieut. HOPE.	
	18		Cadre pass through Baths etc. & are issued with clean changes after which the party moves to No 2 Embarkation Camp, No. 5 WING	

40 M
2 shts.

(12340) Wt W5300/P713 750,000 3/18 D. D. & L., London, E.C. 2688 Forms/C2118/16.

Instructions regarding War Diaries and Intelligence Summaries are contained in F. S. Regs., Part II. and the Staff Manual respectively. Title pages will be prepared in manuscript.

WAR DIARY
or
INTELLIGENCE SUMMARY.
(*Erase heading not required.*)

Army Form C. 2118.

Place	Date	Hour	Summary of Events and Information	Remarks and references to Appendices
DUNKIRK	1919 Apl. 19		Cadre embark on S.S. "MOGILEFF" about 10.30 A.M. and sail for TILBURY about 14.00 hours.	
	20		Arrive TILBURY about 1500 hours, entraining for RIPON at the Docks Station & leaving at 2000 hours.	
	21		Arrive RIPON about 0800 hours, proceeding to No 22 Camp North, pending final Demobilization.	
	22		In Camp in RIPON	
	23		"	
	24		"	
	25		" 27 O.R. of Cadre sent for Demobilization	
	26		"	
	27		"	
	28		"	
	29		" Remainder of Cadre demobilized	

A Campbell Capt.
a/Adj. for C.O.

D. D. & L., London, E.C.
(10340) W1 W5300/P713 750,000 3/18 E 2688 Forms/C2118/16.

15. A. A. POSITIONS & MOUNTINGS. manned by this unit will be handed over on the proper pro-forma, and receipts taken and forwarded by Details to Brigade.

16. TRENCH STORES ETC.
All A. A. Positions, Hot Food Containers, Soyer Stoves, Trench Stores, S.O.S. Signals, Flares, Defence Schemes, Maps and Air Photographs etc. will be taken over and receipts given. List of Stores taken over will reach Battalion Headquarters before dawn on the 8th.

17. BRIGADE WIRING PARTY.
A party of 1 Officer and 50 O.R. will be supplied from Details and will be accommodated in CANDLE TRENCH from 7/8th inst.
Party will be supplied from Surplus Personnel as follows:-

"B" Company. - 25
"D" do - 25

Lieut. Hunter is detailed to take charge of this party. He will report to representative of 106th T.M. Battery at Junction of BEAR TRENCH and CANDLE TRENCH at 2 p.m. 7th, who will allot accommodation.

18. DETAILS.
Details will be accommodated in WELLINGTON Camp under command of Lieut. Stewart.
Parade in full marching order at 3 p.m. on Football Field.
Advance Party will report to Brigade Billeting Officer at 10 a.m. tomorrow at MANNING CAMP.

19. COMPLETION OF RELIEF. will be reported to Battalion Headquarters by code word "BLIGHTY".

(sd) S. Campbell, Lieut. & A/Adjt.
12th High. L. I.

www.ingramcontent.com/pod-product-compliance
Lightning Source LLC
Chambersburg PA
CBHW081544160426
43191CB00011B/1839
* 9 7 8 1 4 7 4 5 1 7 4 1 6 *